Boy
of the Pyramids

A Mystery of Ancient Egypt

Ruth Fosdick Jones

Illustrated by Dorothy Bayley Morse

RANDOM HOUSE
New York

For my children—
Debby, Rufus and Candy

Boy of the Pyramids

A Mystery of Ancient Egypt

At any time and in any place, when there is a mystery to be solved, a ten-year-old boy will want to have a hand in it So it was with Kaffe, an Egyptian boy of long ago.

With his friend Sari, a slave-girl, Kaffe had many adventures—the harvest feast, the fight of the bulls, the flood. Then came the mystery of the pyramid's missing jewels and a dark night when Kaffe, his father, and Sari set out to catch the thief.

Contents

1 Fourteen Copper Rings   3

2 The Slave Market   14

3 Red Boy   30

4 The Harvest   40

5 The Flood   60

6 At Gizeh   79

7 The Green Stone   93

8 Sneferu's Pyramid   108

9 The End of It All   129

1

Fourteen Copper Rings

The sun, rising over the desert cliffs, shone across the green valley of Egypt and the broad River Nile right into Kaffe's eyes. It woke him up, and Kaffe didn't like to be waked that way. He scowled. Then he sat up in bed with his eyes still shut tight. "Num!" he called. "Num!"

There was no answer, so he tried again, louder this time: "Num, draw the curtains!"

Still no answer came. Suddenly Kaffe heard something that sounded very much like a snore. He forgot that he was going to stay sleepy so that he could take another nap after Num had drawn the curtains to keep out the sun. He opened his eyes and bounced out of bed, and there was Num, his black body shining in the sunlight, snoring peacefully on the reed mat at the foot of Kaffe's bed.

"Num," cried Kaffe. "Get up!" He put out his foot to give the Negro a kick in the ribs. People weren't considerate of their servants long ago in Egypt, and anyway, Num was a slave. He wasn't used to consideration.

But Kaffe's foot stopped short just before it touched Num's ribs. Beyond the slave was a cedarwood chair, and folded carefully on the chair was Kaffe's kilt of fine white linen. Not his everyday kilt, but his best one, with his copper-and-turquoise collar laid on top of it.

When he saw that, Kaffe remembered everything and forgot to be cross because Num had overslept and let the sun shine in his eyes. For this was the day his father

4

was taking him to Memphis to spend the copper rings he had been saving.

Altogether, Kaffe had fourteen copper rings. He was very rich for a ten-year-old Eygptian boy. That was because his father had given him two fields. The harvest from them belonged to Kaffe, and his father had paid him eight copper rings for his first harvest, and six for his second. And that very morning he was going to the great city of Memphis to spend the copper rings, all fourteen of them.

With a whoop Kaffe bounded over Num, out of his room, through the house and into the garden. By the time Num had risen sleepily to his feet wondering what all the noise was about, Kaffe was splashing joyfully in the garden pool.

He wondered what he could buy for fourteen copper rings. He had never bought anything before.

"Let's see," he said aloud. "I might buy a new ball. A husk ball covered with leather. But that wouldn't cost very much. Maybe I could get one of the wooden bakers that kneads dough if you pull a string—or I could get Mother a new bracelet."

Then suddenly he had an idea, such a wonderful idea

5

that he dove under water and kicked his feet in the air. "I shall buy a dagger," he said to himself. "One with a gold handle and a flint blade, or maybe a copper blade. A real dagger." None of the boys he knew had one, but then, none of them owned two fields like Kaffe. "And," he added, "if it doesn't cost too much, I'll get the wooden baker, too."

Blowing and sputtering, Kaffe stuck his head out of water, only to have it pushed swiftly under again. "What——," he began as soon as he could speak.

"Look out," said a voice above him, "or the crocodile will get you!"

Kaffe winked the water out of his eyes. His father, Socharis, was standing on the edge of the pool. "And I suppose it was the crocodile who ducked me," answered Kaffe, laughing. Then he saw his father's kilt, all freshly pleated, and his newly curled wig, and the black, false beard that Socharis wore whenever he went away any-where. "Oh, Father," Kaffe cried, "you are ready to go. You'll wait for me, won't you?" He scrambled out of the pool.

"There is no hurry," answered Socharis. "We shall eat our breakfast here while you dry yourself in the sun." He

6

clapped his hands. Almost like magic a slave appeared, carrying a big bowl of dates, figs, bananas and grapes. Behind him came two more slaves, one with a bowl of milk for Kaffe, and the other with a plate of wheat cakes. This was their breakfast.

"Now, Kaffe," said his father when they had finished, "as soon as you are dressed, we can start. I shall tell the slaves to get the boat ready."

Kaffe ran into the house and burst into his room. Num was there waiting to hand him his kilt and necklace and help strap on his papyrus sandals. That was all Kaffe wore, so it did not take him long to get dressed. He was ready in almost as short a time as it takes to tell it.

On a little stand near the door was an ebony box with a border of lotus and papyrus flowers carved around the sides and the figures of the god and goddess of the Nile on the top. In this box Kaffe kept his copper rings. He opened it and counted them to be sure that they were all there, then snatched it up and ran from the room. At the garden door he stopped. Just outside two people were talking, and they were talking about him.

"It is a great deal of money for a little boy to spend." That was Nasha, his mother. Kaffe sighed. He thought he had better not tell her about wanting to buy a dagger. He didn't think she would like it.

"Now, don't worry, Nasha," he heard his father say. "It will turn out all right."

"I hope so," she answered. "But don't let him spend all those rings foolishly, will you, Socharis?"

"Certainly not. Certainly not," replied Socharis. "Where is that boy?" he asked, looking around.

"Here I am, Father," called Kaffe, running out of the house. "Good morning, Mother."

"Good morning, Son." Nasha bent down to kiss him. One hand, with the fingers dyed henna color, rested lightly on his shoulder. Kaffe thought she was very beautiful. Her hair, without her wig, was short and black like his. The green paint around her eyes made them look very large and dark, and she wore a soft green robe over her white linen dress.

"What are you going to buy in Memphis, Kaffe?" she asked.

Kaffe had been afraid she would ask that. "Oh, something very fine," he answered. "It's to be a surprise. You'll see when we get home." He hopped first on one foot, then on the other. "Can we go now, Father?" he asked.

8

"Yes, I think the boat is ready." Socharis picked up his gold-headed staff and turned to leave.

"Good-bye, Mother," shouted Kaffe, and tore down the garden path to the big stone gateway on the river bank before Nasha had time to ask any more questions.

Beyond the gateway was the boat. It was a very gay boat. The rails and even the big steering oar were painted brightly in blue and red and black and white. In the stern was a painted canopy under which Socharis and Kaffe could sit out of the sun. Twelve slaves were already bowed over their oars in the middle of the boat, and as Socharis came down the steps, other slaves were making fast a smaller boat with a cloth-covered cabin that they would tow down the river after them. This was the kitchen boat, and on it were still more slaves and reed baskets of food to be cooked for their dinner.

Socharis stepped on board and sat down under the canopy. Num followed with the litter they would need to carry them through the streets of Memphis. The steersman shouted an order, the slaves pulled on the oars and began their singsong chant, and the boat swung out into the river.

Kaffe looked back at the shore. Only the tops of the

9

trees and the awning over the flat roof of the house showed above the high garden wall. Outside the wall were fields where many slaves were working in the hot sun. There was one field quite near the river with a big fig tree growing in the very center. That was one of Kaffe's fields. His other field was next to it, farther away from the river, and far off behind them both rose the yellow cliffs at the valley's edge. Beyond them was the desert.

Soon the house and the field with the fig tree in the center were hidden from sight behind a bend in the river. Kaffe sat down beside Socharis on a low stool. "Where are we going first when we get to Memphis?" he asked.

He hoped his father would say that he could decide, but Socharis said, "I have an errand to do at the slave market. I need a new field hand and another woman for your mother."

"Oh," said Kaffe. He was disappointed. He did not like to go to the slave market. Sometimes the slaves cried when they were separated from their families. This often happened when one man wanted one part of a family and another man wanted another part. Kaffe wondered if the trip to Memphis was going to be as much fun as he had thought.

But it was pleasant on the river. They passed little villages and houses like the one Kaffe lived in, and tall marshes of papyrus plants. These were reeds from which paper and ropes and sandals were made. Then there were all kinds of boats to watch. One that sailed past them carried a mummy case painted in bright colors and decorated with gold. This was a funeral boat and the mummy case was a coffin made in the shape of a man's figure. The slaves that rowed the boat were chanting mournfully.

"Are they going to Gizeh where Khufu is building his pyramid, Father?" asked Kaffe. Khufu was the pharaoh of Egypt, the king who ruled over the whole Nile valley and all the people in it down to the very last slave. Most of the rich noblemen of the country were buried around the great tomb that he was building for himself.

"Yes. They probably are going to Gizeh," said Socharis in answer to Kaffe's question.

After the funeral boat had passed them, they met a nobleman whom Socharis knew, bound up the river for a picnic. Then they began to see fishing boats floating down to the marshes at the river's mouth, and trading boats from far up the Nile, low in the water with their cargoes of ivory and ebony and gold. As they drew near Memphis, the river seemed alive with boats. It was fun to be with Socharis, because he could always tell what a boat had in it if he knew where it came from.

Kaffe pointed to a big boat. "Where is that one from?" he asked. He knew that it must have come from far away, for it was big enough to have a mast and sail as well as oars.

"It has come from Syria with a load of cedarwood," answered Socharis. "You can smell it, Kaffe." And Kaffe could. The air was spicy with the smell of the wood.

"That smaller boat over there," Socharis went on, "brings copper from Sinai." Soon he had told Kaffe where all the boats came from and what goods they were carrying.

All the bigger boats seemed to be trying to land at once. Sailors shouted at each other, oars scraped together, and every so often there was the sharp snap of an overseer's whip on a slave's bare back. Socharis' boat threaded its way toward shore. The slaves shipped their oars, and the boat slid quietly up to the landing stairs.

Then the litter was set down on the ground so that Socharis and Kaffe could step in. This was a kind of chair that was carried on poles by four slaves, and there was plenty of room in it for Kaffe and Socharis to sit side by side. When they had settled themselves comfortably, the slaves picked up the carrying poles and away they went toward the market place with Num running ahead to clear a way for them through the narrow, crowded streets.

2

The Slave Market

The slave market was a big square crowded with groups
of slaves bound with ropes. From group to group moved
the people who had come to buy them. They looked the
slaves over carefully. They made them stand up,

14

thumped them here and there, and felt their muscles. People who bought slaves wanted strong men and women who could work hard. If they bought sick slaves, they spent their money poorly.

"What kind of slaves are you going to buy, Father?" asked Kaffe. "Are you going to get some more Nubians like Num?" Negroes were called Nubians in Egypt because the name of the country from which they came was Nubia.

"No, I think I shall try Sand People this time," said Socharis casually.

"Sand People?" asked Kaffe. "Where do they come from?"

"Some of them live near Sinai," answered Socharis. "I saw them there when I went to see Khufu's copper mines."

"What do they look like?" asked Kaffe. "Are they black like Num?"

"No. They are not very different from us."

Just then another nobleman came up and greeted Socharis. His name was Anhotep. He had small, shifty black eyes and thin, cruel lips. Kaffe didn't like the man's looks, but when his father said to Anhotep, "This is my son, Oserkaf," Kaffe spoke to him politely, as he had been taught.

Oserkaf was Kaffe's real name, but it was used only on special occasions. Kaffe was so much easier to say.

Anhotep bowed, but Kaffe noticed that even when his lips smiled, his eyes did not. "He is a fine boy, Socharis," said the nobleman, and patted Kaffe on the head. Kaffe liked him even less after that. He was much too old, he thought, to be patted on the head. People did that only to babies and dogs.

"You are buying more slaves, Socharis?" asked Anhotep.

"Yes. I need a new field hand, and a woman for Nasha."

"You will get Nubians, I suppose," said Anhotep. "You chose well when you bought that one," he added, looking admiringly at Num who stood behind Socharis fanning the flies away.

"No," said Socharis. "I think I shall buy Sand People this time. I am curious to see what kind of slaves they make."

"Sand People?" cried Anhotep. "Then I know just the pair for you. Come with me."

As they walked slowly across the square Anhotep explained, "These slaves I spoke of just now—there is a family. Father, mother and little girl. The father and mother might do for you. I am not interested in them, but wait until you see the child. She would make a perfect dancing girl." They had reached the other side of the square now. Kaffe saw tall people all around him. Their skin was lighter than that of the Egyptians, and many of them had curly hair.

Anhotep stopped before a ragged man and woman kneeling side by side on the ground. The man was fine looking, but he was very thin and had the saddest eyes Kaffe had ever seen. The woman was thin and sad, too. Both of them looked frightened. The woman held close in her arms what Kaffe thought was a large bundle, and when anyone came near or even looked at her, she clutched it more tightly.

"See, Socharis," Anhotep said. "Isn't she a beauty?" He pulled the bundle roughly from the woman's arms and jerked it to its feet. What Kaffe thought was a bundle was not a bundle at all. It was a little girl about his own age. She tried to pull away from Anhotep and run back to her mother, but the nobleman held her fast

He put his hand under her chin and tipped her head back so that Socharis could see her face. Kaffe saw it, too. She was beautiful. She had big dark eyes, and her hair, which was very curly, tumbled all around her little heart-shaped face.

"In a year or two when she is trained—why, Socharis, people will fight to come to my parties just to see her!"

"Ummm," said Socharis thoughtfully. Kaffe wondered if his father was thinking the same thing he was. He hated to have Anhotep buy the little girl.

"Father," he began, but Anhotep interrupted him.

"What do you say, Socharis?" he said. "You take the man and woman and I'll take the girl. In that way we can buy the whole family between us."

"The man and woman might do very well for me," said Socharis. "They are pretty thin but good food will cure that."

"But, Father," cried Kaffe. "The little girl. Can't you get her, too?"

"Anhotep is buying her, Kaffe," Socharis reminded him.

"But they ought to go together, the whole family. You

mustn't let Anhotep buy her away from her father and mother."

Anhotep had beckoned to a slave dealer and again snatched the child from her mother. The whole family understood what was being done then. The little girl shrieked and clung to her mother, the woman wailed, and there were tears even in the man's eyes. Anhotep paid no attention to the noise. He took the child from her family and dragged her before the slave dealer.

Kaffe couldn't bear it. "Oh, Father," he cried, "you mustn't let him have her."

Socharis looked very much upset. "I should like to get her, Kaffe," he said, "but Anhotep would be very angry He saw her first, you know."

"But you wouldn't want us to be separated if we were slaves," insisted Kaffe.

"I know. I know," said Socharis helplessly.

"Is Anhotep a very powerful noble?" asked Kaffe in a discouraged voice. It did not do to make powerful nobles angry.

"Well, no," said Socharis, "but even so——"

They could hear Anhotep quarreling with the dealer

over the price of the child. Beside them her father and mother wailed pitifully.

Kaffe made up his mind. "Father," he said, tugging at Socharis' kilt. "You told me, didn't you, that I could buy anything I wanted with my copper rings?"

"Yes, Kaffe," said his father.

"Then," said Kaffe, "I am going to buy that little girl." And he dashed off before Socharis had time to say anything.

"I will give you four rings," Anhotep was saying as Kaffe came up to him.

"You will rob me, Master," moaned the slave dealer.

Kaffe's heart was in his mouth. "I will give five," he said loudly.

Anhotep turned around. He was very much surprised when he saw who was bidding against him.

"Six! Six!" whined the dealer.

"All right. Six!" said Anhotep. He scowled at Kaffe.

"Seven," said Kaffe.

"Eight," shouted Anhotep angrily.

"Nine," said Kaffe.

Just then he felt a hand on his shoulder. Socharis was standing behind him. "I have bought the father and mother," he said in a voice too low for Anhotep to hear. "Keep bidding, Kaffe. I doubt if he will want to go much higher."

"Ten," said Anhotep to the dealer. Then turning to Socharis, he said, "I hold it ill done of you to bid against me. I should think that your gratitude to me for showing you that fine pair of slaves would have kept you from it."

Socharis shook his head. "You do not understand, Anhotep," he replied. "It is not I who am bidding against you, but my son, here. He does not approve of separating families, and since I have bought the child's father and mother, he wishes to buy her."

"Eleven," said Kaffe promptly.

Anhotep did not even reply to Socharis' speech. "Twelve," he said to the dealer. His face was red and angry and it was plain to see that he thought Socharis had got Kaffe to bid for the slave girl because he wanted her himself.

"Thirteen," said Kaffe. He was worried now. If Anhotep bid again, Kaffe did not have enough money to overbid him unless he could borrow from his father on the next harvest, and he hated to have to do that in front of Anhotep.

But Anhotep was frowning at the brick pavement. He was thinking hard. At last he looked up at Socharis. "It is plain," he said, "that you would stake the boy to any price, so I am wasting my time. I shall withdraw." And before Kaffe realized what was happening Anhotep had bowed and walked off.

"Fourteen. Fourteen," begged the dealer, holding out his hand.

Kaffe shook his head. "Thirteen is all I shall pay," he said boldly. "Here is your money." He opened his ebony box and counted the rings into the man's hand.

"I am afraid that you have made an enemy, Kaffe," said Socharis.

Kaffe thought so, too, but he asked, "Aren't you glad I bought her, Father?"

Socharis smiled. "Very glad, Son," he said.

"Now," said Kaffe, "we must make them understand that they belong to us and can live together and be happy."

He took the little girl by the hand. "Come on," he cried, forgetting that she did not understand a word he said. "Let's tell your father and mother." He pulled her after him to the place where the man and woman still

22

waited sorrowfully. Their happiness knew no bounds when they understood that they would not be separated after all.

Socharis and Kaffe got into the litter and the three new slaves, with Num to watch them, followed on foot. As they made their way through the streets they passed a shop where toys were sold. It was not like our shops, for it was just a little hole-in-the-wall sort of place, so small that the toys seemed to have overflowed from it. Most of them were outside in the street under a canopy.

"Oh, Father," cried Kaffe when he saw the shop, "may I stop here just for a minute?"

His father smiled. "To spend the other copper ring?" he asked.

"Yes," said Kaffe. "Only it's for the little girl, not for me."

Socharis ordered the litter to be set down and Kaffe ran into the shop. When he came out a few minutes later, he held in his hand a very queer-looking object. It was a flat piece of wood, shaped like a paddle, with a necklace and skirt painted on it. Attached to a knob at one end were many strings of mud beads, and on the knob itself was painted something that looked like a face. Anyway, there were two black eyes with large white circles painted around them.

Kaffe ran to the little slave girl. "Here is a doll for you," he said. For this strange thing was an Egyptian doll. The little girl took it wonderingly and turned it over and over, then hugged it tightly to her and smiled at Kaffe. He smiled, too, and started back toward the litter. Then he suddenly thought of something. He went back to the little girl. "What is your name?" he asked.

The little girl looked puzzled. She shook her head. Kaffe realized that she did not know what he had said to her. He pointed to himself. "Kaffe," he said.

Then he pointed to her. "You?" he asked.

She understood. "Sari," she said, pointing to herself. Then, pointing to him, she said, "Kaffe."

They both laughed.

Socharis called from the litter. Kaffe jumped in beside him and they started once more toward the boat landing.

While they had been away, the slaves on the kitchen boat had been very busy. When the litter was set down, Kaffe smelled delicious odors. He realized that he was

Kaffe and Sari stood at the rail

hungry. He and Socharis sat down under the canopy, and the slaves served them with all the good things they had been cooking. From where he sat, Kaffe watched Sari, and her father, whose name was Ben, and her mother, whose name was Neemat. They sat in the bow of the boat eating their lunch. They ate as though they were hungry and talked in low voices between bites.

Afterwards, while the slaves rowed them up the river against the current, Kaffe and Sari stood at the rail watching the banks slide past them. Kaffe showed her crocodiles lying on the shore in the sun, and pink lotus flowers and tall, green papyrus plants. Once they saw a fat hippopotamus wallowing in a marsh, and farther on, a flock of wild ducks rose quickly into the air as they passed.

It was late in the afternoon when Kaffe said to Sari, "Look! You can see our villa there over the tops of those trees." Country houses like the one Kaffe lived in were called villas. Something white fluttered from a corner of the flat roof. That, Kaffe knew, was Nasha waving to them. He jumped up and down with excitement.

As soon as the boat reached the landing stairs, he dragged Sari after him through the garden and up the

26

outside stairs to the roof. Socharis followed more slowly, and last of all came Num with Ben and Neemat.

"Look, Mother," cried Kaffe. "See what I bought with thirteen of my copper rings. And I bought her a doll with the other one," he added proudly.

Nasha stared. "Do you mean to say that you bought a girl slave?" she asked in amazement.

"Yes," said Kaffe. "You see I had to——" He was just going to explain why he had to when Socharis reached the head of the stairs.

"Socharis," cried Nasha, "did you let Kaffe buy a slave girl after promising me——"

"But, Mother," interrupted Kaffe, "if I had not bought her, she never would have seen her mother and father again and Anhotep would have bought her for a dancing girl."

"Dancing girl? Anhotep? What are you talking about?" asked Nasha.

So finally Socharis and Kaffe told Nasha the story of what had happened to Kaffe's fourteen copper rings. Nasha was very much astonished.

"Well!" she said when they had finished. "When you go to Memphis again I shall go with you. A slave girl is

27

at least useful, but next time you might bring home a tame hippopotamus!"

She beckoned Sari to her and turned her around, looking at her carefully. "She is very pretty," she said at last. She smiled at Sari and Sari smiled back at her. Then Sari was prettier than ever.

Nasha turned to Kaffe. "You are quite right, Son," she said. "She is too nice a little girl to be a dancing girl. What you will do with a slave, I cannot imagine, but perhaps I can find some work for her to do if you will let me use her. You must not let her grow up to be a tomboy who does not know how to do anything."

"Yes, Mother," said Kaffe, absently. "May Sari sleep at the foot of my bed, like Num?"

"No, indeed," answered his mother. "She will sleep with her own family in her own house, where she belongs."

"But Mother, she's *my* slave!"

"Why, Kaffe," said Socharis with a twinkle in his eyes, "I thought you were the boy who did not believe in separating families."

Kaffe couldn't think of an answer to that.

"And now, my dear," said Socharis to Nasha, "if you

will come with me I shall show you Sari's father and mother."

They went down the stairs, leaving the two children on the roof.

"I really think it was most kind and thoughtful of Kaffe to spend his money for the little girl," Kaffe heard his mother say, "but of course it wouldn't do to tell him so."

"No, of course not," agreed Socharis.

Kaffe smiled to himself. Parents were very queer, he thought.

3

Red Boy

So it was that Sari and Ben and Neemat came to live in the little mud-brick house not far from Kaffe's fields. Even though they were slaves, they were very happy, for they had plenty of food to eat and a good home and a kind master and mistress.

Soon Ben was strong enough to work all day in the fields. Neemat spent many hours in the little courtyard of their house working at her loom. It was not long before she could weave linen as fine and even as silk. Sometimes Sari helped her by twisting the flax fibers into thread, but most of the time she was up at the villa or off somewhere with Kaffe.

Sari and Kaffe could not talk to each other very much at first because Sari could not speak Egyptian, but she soon learned. When they were out in the fields, Kaffe would point to the plow that the slaves were using and say, "Plow." Sari would repeat it after him, and then they would both laugh at the way she said it. It was not long before she understood everything Kaffe said. "Go and get my ball, Sari," he would say, remembering that she was his slave and that he should be ordering her about. And Sari would run off to find it. Then they would have a game and Kaffe would forget again that she was his slave, and they would just have a good time playing together.

One bright morning they were sitting on the grass under the big fig tree in the center of Kaffe's field. All

31

around them the slaves were working. Kaffe explained to Sari what they were doing.

"You see," he said, "first the slaves have to plow the land. That leaves the earth in big lumps, so they take mallets and pound it fine. Then they water the fields and sow the seed. The men down there at the end of the field are just finishing. They carry the seed in those little baskets. And the men working just behind them are raking soil over the seeds."

"I see," said Sari. "What are they going to do after that?"

"They will get the oxen and drive them all around the field to trample the seeds into the ground." As he said that, Kaffe had an idea. "I know," he cried. "Let's ask Ani if we can go and get the oxen and drive them down here." Ani was the slave who had charge of the farming.

Together the children ran down the field. "I say, Ani," called Kaffe.

"Yes, Master Kaffe." Ani smiled at the two children.

"May we get the oxen for you?" asked Kaffe. "You will soon be ready to use them."

"Why, yes," said Ani good-naturedly. "You may if you want to. Only remember," he called after them as they ran off, "Red Boy is in that pasture, too, so be sure to fasten the gate." Red Boy was Socharis' prize bull, and he was very fond of getting out through unlatched gates.

"We'll remember," Kaffe promised.

It was quite a long way to the pasture, and it was hard walking over the freshly plowed ground. By the time they reached the pasture both children were hot and tired, so they climbed up on the gate and sat there to cool off.

"See," said Kaffe, "there is Red Boy down at the other end of the pasture. Red Boy! Red Boy!" he called.

Red Boy raised his head, rolled one eye at Kaffe and Sari, and then went back to his grazing. He was a handsome bull, all reddish brown except for a white streak on his nose and a broad white patch on his chest.

"He's the best fighting bull around here," boasted Kaffe. "You'll see him fight at harvest time. He's wonderful."

"What does he fight?" asked Sari. She glanced at Red Boy's smooth horns. They looked very sharp.

"Other bulls, of course," said Kaffe. "What did you think he fought? Crocodiles?"

33

"I just wondered," said Sari. Red Boy had raised his head again and stood gazing at them. He looked very fierce. "Do you have to go into the pasture to get the oxen?" she asked.

"Oh, no," said Kaffe. "You do it like this." He picked a handful of grass that was growing beside the gate. "You pick some, too," he said to Sari. He leaned over the gate and held out the grass. "Here, Sut! Here, Nep!" he called. "They know their names," he explained, "and they'll come to get the grass."

The two oxen lumbered slowly toward the gate, and Kaffe kept calling them and waving his handful of grass at them. Sari waved hers and called, too. Finally Kaffe opened the gate and the two great beasts lumbered through.

"Look out, Sari! Don't let him go into the garden," warned Kaffe as Nep started off toward the vegetable garden. "He's very fond of lettuce and he'll trample everything. Show him the grass and he'll follow you."

Sari did as she was told, but Nep had made up his mind to have lettuce and paid no attention to her.

"Wait. I'll get him," called Kaffe, slamming the gate behind him. It made a loud noise and sounded as if it

34

were closed, and Kaffe was in a hurry so he didn't look to see.

He caught up with Nep and kicked him gently. After that Nep abandoned the idea of lettuce, and both oxen trotted off toward Kaffe's field with the two children running in front of them, urging them on with their bunches of grass.

Red Boy watched them go. Perhaps his feelings were hurt because he had been left behind with the rams and cows, or perhaps he just wanted to see where Sut and Nep were going. Anyway, he walked slowly to the gate and hung his head over it. Then he lowered his head and pushed the gate gently. Nothing happened, so he pushed harder, and still a little harder, and the gate swung open!

Red Boy poked his nose through, then his shoulders, and pretty soon all of him was on the other side. He was a little surprised, but it was pleasant to be outside the pasture. He flicked the flies away with his tail and started off after Sut and Nep and the children. The farther he got from the pasture the friskier he felt. He pawed up some earth. Then he felt still better. He began to run.

Kaffe and Sari had reached the field when Sari happened to look behind her, and there was Red Boy tearing over the rough ground, his head lowered, kicking his heels in the air. Sari screamed and Kaffe turned to see what was the matter. He didn't waste any time screaming. He just seized Sari's hand and ran as fast as he could for the fig tree. He shouted as he ran, "Ani! Ani! Red Boy is loose!"

Red Boy heard the screaming and shouting. To him they meant only one thing, and that thing was a fight. Everybody screamed and shouted when he fought. So he looked around for something to fight, and there were two little figures running as fast as they could away from him. The slaves were running, too, but Red Boy saw Kaffe and Sari first, so he started after them.

The plowed ground was hard to run on, and Red Boy could run much faster than Sari and Kaffe could. It seemed to them that he must surely overtake them before they got to the tree. Twice Sari slipped and almost fell, but Kaffe pulled her up and they stumbled on. At last, when Sari thought she could not run another step, Kaffe reached up, grasped a branch of the tree, and scrambled up, half dragging Sari after him.

36

They were not a moment too soon. Red Boy reached the tree only a few seconds after they did. He was enraged because the children had got away from him. He tore up the grass under the tree and ran at the trunk with his horns. Then he gave it up and rushed off around the field, bellowing as he went.

Kaffe was nearly in tears. "Look! Look what he's doing to my field!" he wailed.

Sari wailed, too, and what with the slaves shouting and Red Boy bellowing and everybody running from all directions giving orders, there was quite a commotion. Every time a slave tried to catch Red Boy, he would lower his horns and run right at the man, and the slave would have to run away and jump the ditch that surrounded the field to save himself.

At last Kaffe saw his father coming across the fields with his mother and Neemat close behind. As soon as he reached the next field, Socharis ordered everybody to stop trying to catch Red Boy. They let him caper around the field until he was tired out. Then Ben slipped a halter over the bull's neck and led him out of the field and back to the pasture. After that everybody ran to the fig tree.

37

"Are you all right?" called Nasha and Socharis and Neemat at the same time.

"Yes," said Kaffe and Sari from their perch among the branches.

Nasha sighed with relief. She was so glad that the children were not hurt that she laughed and said, "Well, if you don't look like two frightened wild fowls up there! Come down."

Kaffe and Sari looked down at the ground. It seemed a long way off. "We can't get down," they cried. "It's too far."

Socharis chuckled. "Then how did you get up?" he asked.

"I don't know," wailed Kaffe. "We didn't have time to think about it."

Everybody laughed and someone reached up and helped them down. Then they all walked back to the villa.

Nothing was said about Red Boy until after they had eaten their lunch. Then when they were sitting out in the arbor Kaffe said, "It was my fault, Father, that Red Boy got out. I didn't fasten the gate."

"Ummm," said Socharis. "You know that your field will have to be planted all over again, Kaffe."

"Yes," replied Kaffe unhappily.

"That means," said Socharis, "that I shall have to give you more seed. I can't afford to have seed wasted because a bull tears up your field. What do you think we had better do about it?"

Kaffe thought hard for a minute. "Well," he said at last, "if you will trust me until the harvest, I will give you one of my copper rings to pay for the seed. Will that be all right?"

Socharis nodded. "Yes. I think that will be satisfactory," he said.

"And," promised Kaffe, "I'll never, never leave that gate open again!"

"No, I don't believe you will," said his father comfortingly.

4

The Harvest

The days went by so swiftly that it was hard to tell them apart, and all the time the grain was growing steadily taller and more golden. Even the wheat in the field that Red Boy had trampled grew well, and all over the land slaves worked from morning to night watering the fields.

Finally, one afternoon when all the family was sitting in the garden, Ani came and knelt before Socharis. "See, Master," he said. "The grain is ripe." He held in his hands a full yellow ear of wheat.

"Good," said Socharis. "Then we will begin to harvest tomorrow."

The next morning Kaffe and Sari were in the fields while the sun was still low in the east. But early as they were, the slaves were there before them. The curved blades of their sickles flashed in the sun as they worked. As soon as they finished cutting the grain, other slaves bound the stalks into sheaves and packed them into baskets which they loaded on the backs of donkeys. Then women and children picked up all the heads of grain that had been broken off in harvesting. Nothing was ever wasted in Egypt. There were too many hungry people to be fed.

When the patient little donkeys were loaded, they were led off to the threshing floor. This was a large square of hard-packed earth. Kaffe and Sari followed

41

the donkey train and were just in time to see the first grain of the harvest dumped upon the floor.

"What do they do that for?" asked Sari.

"You'll see," answered Kaffe. "They are bringing Sut and Nep now." One of the slaves drove the two oxen straight onto the threshing floor, and then round and round it and back and forth until the stalks of grain were all crushed and broken.

"What a queer thing to do!" exclaimed Sari.

"No, it isn't," Kaffe told her. "They have to do that to separate the kernels of grain from the stalks."

"But it can't be separated! Look at it," said Sari.

"They haven't finished yet," said Kaffe patiently.

Six women slaves with white cloths tied around their heads walked out on the threshing floor. Each one carried two curved paddles in her hands. They began to pick up the grain on the paddles and toss it into the air. A little breeze was blowing. It carried away all the dust and broken stalks, but the heavy kernels of grain fell back on the floor. When they had finished, only a pile of clean kernels was left.

Day after day the harvesting went on, and each night saw more grain stored away in the granary.

"It won't take many more days to finish," said Kaffe one afternoon as they went back to the villa. "Let's ask Father when the harvest holiday will be."

"What's a holiday?" asked Sari.

"Why, a day when nobody works and we all take gifts to the temple and there are feasts and everybody has a good time."

They found Socharis and Nasha in the arbor. Socharis was reading a letter which was written on thin strips of papyrus pasted together. The writing looked like a lot of little black pictures.

"Father," called Kaffe as soon as he saw his father and mother, "when is the holiday going to be?"

"A week from today," answered Socharis.

"Whom is your letter from?" asked Nasha as the two children came up.

"From Anhotep," said Socharis.

"What does he want?" asked Nasha.

"He wants to bring his new bull to fight Red Boy when he comes to the harvest feast," answered Socharis.

"Did you invite Anhotep to the feast?" asked Kaffe in surprise.

"Yes," answered Socharis, smiling. "I thought it might

43

make him feel better about your taking Sari right out from under his nose."

"And are you going to let him bring his bull?" asked Kaffe.

"I don't know what to do about that," said Socharis. "I am almost sure Red Boy will win, for he is the best bull in this part of Egypt, and Anhotep wouldn't like that."

"But," said Nasha, "Anhotep suggested it himself, so it will be his own fault if his bull is beaten."

"That's so," agreed Socharis. "I suppose I may as well let him bring the bull. It's a new one Anhotep has just bought, and of course he wants to try him out. But I hope Red Boy will not beat him too badly," he added.

The next week passed very slowly. Kaffe and Sari thought the holiday would never come, but of course it finally did. And what an exciting day it was!

Everybody at the villa and everybody in all the little mud-brick houses where the slaves lived was up very early that morning. They all ran back and forth on errands and got in each other's way, and they were all very gay and nobody minded in the least. At last Socharis and Nasha and Kaffe, with Sari beside him, came out of

the villa and stepped into their litters. The slaves formed
a long line behind them and they all set off, carrying the
gifts that Socharis was going to take to the temple to
offer to the gods in thanks for the good harvest.

There were so many measures of wheat, and so many
lengths of fine linen, and so many jars of honey and but-
ter and olive oil, and so many live geese and ducks—and
even cows and goats—and so many slaves to carry them
all, that it made a very long procession indeed. When
the end of it was just leaving the villa, Socharis
and Nasha and Kaffe and Sari were already turning into
the road that led to the temple.

Along the road, people from the nearby villages
joined them and made the procession even longer. Everyone was talking and laughing, and the geese were
cackling and the cattle lowing. The priests heard them
coming and met them at the temple gate, their white
linen headdresses and kilts and gold collars shining in
the sun. They led the procession into the courtyard, took
the gifts and carried them into the temple, where they
offered them to the gods. Outside, in the courtyard,
the people prayed and sang and watched the temple
dancers as they danced in honor of the gods.

Afterwards, the priests came from the temple and greeted Socharis, and while he and Nasha talked to them, Kaffe and Sari wandered around the courtyard. Sari had never seen such a big and beautiful place. Above was the blue Egyptian sky, and around the sides of the courtyard were thick stone pillars painted in bright colors. On the walls behind these were pictures of the gods and goddesses the Egyptians worshiped, so large that they made the children feel very small just to look at them.

There was Hathor, the Cow Goddess, and Horus with his hawk's head, and a round disc with beautifully colored wings on either side that Kaffe told Sari was Re, the Sun God. Then there was Keb, the Earth God, lying on his back with trees and flowers growing from him, and above him was Nut, the Sky Goddess, her body arched and her dress all covered with stars. By the time the two children had been around the courtyard once, Socharis and Nasha were ready to go, and the procession, empty-handed, started home.

The trip to the temple was only the beginning of that wonderful day. Almost as soon as Kaffe's family reached home, their guests began to arrive for the feast. They came in litters, carried by their slaves, dressed in fine white linen clothes and bright jewels and curled black wigs.

At last, when it seemed as though everyone in Egypt must be there, the children saw another litter coming, and behind it, slaves leading a great bull. Kaffe gasped when he saw the bull, for he was enormous. He snorted and shook his head from side to side as he came, and he was coal black from his nose to the tip of his tail.

Anhotep stepped out of the litter at the door and greeted Socharis and Nasha. Then he saw Kaffe and Sari. "Well, Master Oserkaf," he said to Kaffe, "are you still satisfied with your slave?"

"Yes, sir," answered Kaffe.

"I thought you chose well," said Anhotep. "And now she is strong and rosy and prettier than ever." He smiled with great good humor, and nobody seeing him would ever believe that he had been angry at Kaffe for buying Sari. Kaffe found it hard to believe himself.

Anhotep then turned to Socharis and waved his hand toward the bull. "How do you like him, Socharis?" he asked.

"He is magnificent," said Socharis. "I am afraid that

47

Red Boy will have a hard time to hold his own with such a one to fight. What do you call him?"

"The Nubian," answered Anhotep. "I think he is indeed a fit opponent for Red Boy. That bull of yours has never met his match before. This should be a treat for your guests. Do you not agree?"

"It should be, indeed," answered Socharis. He clapped his hands to summon the slaves. "We shall have him put into a pen until after we have refreshed ourselves with such poor food as the house affords," he said courteously, bowing to his guest. He ordered the slaves to take the Nubian to the pen, then led Anhotep through the house and into the garden.

The garden looked very different from the way it did on ordinary days. There were rich rugs spread on the grass, and carved chairs with soft cushions in them set around in a big circle. Wonderful odors floated out through the open kitchen door, and slaves hurried to and fro with trays and bowls piled high with good things to eat. These they set on low stools where all could reach them.

At last everything was ready and everyone sat down to eat. There was no table, and there were no knives and forks and spoons. The guests ate with their fingers and then dipped their hands into copper bowls of water that the slaves passed around. As they dined they listened to the flute players and harpists and watched the graceful dancing girls that Socharis had hired to entertain them.

Finally, when no one could eat another mouthful, Socharis rose from his chair. "My friends," he said, "Anhotep has brought his new bull, the Nubian, to fight Red Boy. If it would please you to see this match, pray come with me."

Kaffe and Sari did not wait to hear any more. They dashed out through the kitchen and ran to the pen where Anhotep's slaves were getting the Nubian ready for the fight. They were fitting smooth wooden balls on the ends of his horns.

"Why do they do that when they are going to fight?" asked Sari.

"Because," answered Kaffe, "nobody wants his bull to be really hurt. This way they just struggle together, and the one that is downed first loses."

"Do you think Red Boy can beat the Nubian?" Sari asked anxiously.

Kaffe looked at the powerful muscles that rippled be-

49

neath the Nubian's black coat. He felt a little doubtful himself, but he would not admit it. "Of course he'll win," he said. "Red Boy has never been beaten."

Just then Num came running up. "Master Kaffe," he called, "your father says that it is time for you to come if you want to see the fight." He led them over to a large enclosed circle. Around it were chairs for the guests so that they could sit at their ease and watch the fight. Kaffe sat down next to Socharis, and Sari sat on the ground at his feet. They had scarcely had time to settle themselves before they saw Anhotep's slaves leading the Nubian from his pen. He was rearing and pawing the earth and lowering his horns at the slaves. Behind him came Socharis' slaves with Red Boy.

When both bulls were safely shut in the ring, the people rose to their feet and cheered and shouted to make them angry. That was not hard to do because both animals had been starved since the day before, and they were naturally fierce anyway. They capered around the ring for a minute or two, then lowered their great heads, bellowed, and ran straight at each other. They struck each other's heads so hard that it seemed as if they must have cracked their skulls, but they only staggered back a step or two, shook themselves, and then circled off to charge again as fiercely as before.

This time they locked horns and struggled and snorted in the middle of the ring until the air was filled with clouds of dust. Time after time they ran at each other while everybody shouted to anger them even further. They reared and plunged, and the ground shook with the pounding of their hoofs as they charged.

"They are indeed well matched," called Socharis to Anhotep above the noise.

Anhotep nodded, but did not take his eyes from the two animals, now about to charge again.

"He looks as if he were watching for something," thought Kaffe to himself.

He heard the sound of running hoofs and turned back to the fight. Red Boy and the Nubian were charging head on. Then Kaffe saw the Nubian duck his head beneath Red Boy's horns and go straight for his broad white chest. To everyone's surprise, Red Boy bellowed with pain and, twisting away, tore around the ring with the Nubian close at his heels. Only as the two bulls came toward them did Kaffe see that the white patch on Red Boy's chest seemed to be shrinking and getting red like

51

Red Boy and the Nubian were charging head on

the rest of his coat. But it was a different shade of red, and suddenly Kaffe realized that Red Boy had been wounded.

Sari tugged at his kilt. "Kaffe, Kaffe," she was crying, "look! The Nubian has lost the ball off one of his horns."

After that nobody knew quite what was happening for a few minutes. There was a great deal of shouting and bellowing and ropes flying through the air and dust in such thick clouds that it was hard to see what was going on. But in the end the slaves managed to rope the two bulls. They took the Nubian back to his pen, still bellowing because he wanted to finish the fight, and they led Red Boy off to the stables, roaring because he was hurt.

The children started off after Red Boy. Just ahead of them were Socharis and Anhotep. They heard Anhotep say, "It was a most unfortunate accident. The slave who fitted the balls on the Nubian's horns shall be well beaten."

When they reached the stables, they found that Red Boy had been tied in his stall, and the slaves were trying to treat his wounded chest. There was a long crimson gash where the Nubian had gored him, and every time anyone tried to touch him Red Boy roared and plunged and shook his horns so that no one could get near him, even though he was tied. And all the time the great gash was bleeding more and more. It seemed as if he would bleed to death if something could not be done soon.

Sari's father, Ben, had come into the stable with the rest. He stood there, watching all that went on. At last he went up to Socharis and spoke to him. "Master," he said, "I have treated many animals in my own country. Perhaps I might be able to treat Red Boy's wound."

Socharis made up his mind quickly. "You have leave to do anything you can, Ben," he said. "No one else seems able to do anything, not even the head of my stables." At that, the slave who had charge of the stables slunk back into the shadows as quickly as he could.

"Thank you, Master," said Ben. "There is just one thing I ask."

"What is that?" asked Socharis.

"That I may be left alone with the bull. Having so many people around excites him as much as the pain of his wound."

"Very well," said Socharis, and led the way out into the sunshine.

54

Socharis and Kaffe went back to the villa and busied themselves for the next few minutes with saying good-bye to their guests. But after everyone had gone—last of all Anhotep with the Nubian behind him—they went back to the stables. Everything there was quiet now. Red Boy had stopped his bellowing. They peeped in at the door. Ben was squatting on the floor waiting for them, and in his stall, Red Boy was contentedly munching hay. There was a broad white linen bandage across his chest.

Socharis smiled. "Well done, Ben," he said. "You have a way with animals. I marked it the day Red Boy treed the children. You would rather care for animals than farm, would you not?"

"Yes, Master, if I had my choice," answered Ben.

"You shall have it," said Socharis. "From now on, you are to have charge of all the animals on my land. When a man has such a gift, it is foolish to waste it in a wheat field."

For the first time since he had lived at the villa, Ben smiled. "It is no hard lot to be a slave with you as master, Socharis," he said. "I thank you, and I shall care for your herds as well as I am able. But before you go," he

55

added, "may I have leave to go back to the ring where the fight was held? I want to look for something."

"Certainly," said Socharis. "What is it you wish to find?"

"I would rather not say until I have found it," said Ben.

"Take us with you!" clamored Kaffe and Sari. Ben sounded very mysterious.

Ben nodded, and Socharis went back to the villa.

"Won't you tell us, Father, what you are looking for?" asked Sari as they reached the ring. "We might help you find it."

Ben opened the gate. "So you might," he said. "I am looking for the ball that came off the Nubian's horn."

"The ball that came off the Nubian's horn!" exclaimed Kaffe. "What do you want to find that for?"

"Because I am a very curious man," answered Ben, and refused to say another word.

For several minutes they searched the ring, shuffling their feet through the soft dust without finding anything. Then Kaffe hit something with his foot. He picked it up. It was half of the wooden ball they were looking for.

"It must have cracked in two when the Nubian charged Red Boy," said Kaffe, handing it to Ben.

Ben rubbed the dirt off the little piece of wood and looked at it carefully. He seemed well pleased with what he saw. "I think your father would like to see this," he said to Kaffe. "Shall we take it to him?"

"But don't you want the other half?" asked Sari.

"We don't need it. This is enough," answered Ben. With the two children beside him almost bursting with curiosity, he started toward the house.

Socharis and Nasha were in the garden. Ben knelt on the grass before Socharis. "Master Kaffe found what I was looking for," he said. "It is part of the ball from the Nubian's horn."

Socharis took the broken ball and turned it over and over. Kaffe hung over his shoulder and Sari hung over Kaffe's shoulder. They all looked at it carefully. The ball had been broken right in half, but along one side of the break was a dark gray line. When he saw that, Kaffe began to understand.

57

"I see," he cried. "The ball was cracked before the Nubian went into the fight. That dark streak is part of the old crack where the wood has weathered and turned gray."

Ben smiled, and Socharis said, "You are right, Kaffe."

"But Anhotep probably didn't know the ball was cracked," said Nasha.

Kaffe remembered how Anhotep had looked as though he were waiting for something when he was watching the fight. "I think he *did* know," Kaffe said excitedly, and told them what he had seen.

"But why should he want to do such a thing?" asked Nasha.

"We do not know that he did," answered Socharis, "and we shall probably never know. He may have been trying to get even with me for letting Kaffe buy Sari."

"But how foolish!" said Nasha.

Socharis sent Ben and Sari away, then rose from his chair and began to pace up and down the garden path. "The thing that puzzles me even more than the matter of the wooden ball," he said, "is where Anhotep got the money to buy a bull like the Nubian. He spent all the wealth his father left him long ago, and he certainly did

58

not have much the day we met him at the slave market, or he would not have hesitated to pay fourteen copper rings for a slave girl."

"Do bulls like the Nubian cost more than slave girls?" asked Kaffe.

"Much more," answered Socharis. "I don't understand it," he muttered half to himself, and started pacing again.

5

The Flood

"How many days is it since the holiday?" asked Sari one morning when she and Kaffe were sitting under the canopy on the roof.

"Seven," said Kaffe. "No, eight. Oh, I don't know. What difference does it make?"

"I just wondered," answered Sari. "It's so hard to count the days. They are all alike. If it rained once in a while it would be easier to remember, because then you could say, 'Two days ago it rained and the feast was three days before that.' But I don't believe it has rained since we came here."

"Of course it hasn't," said Kaffe. "It never rains in Egypt or, at least, not very often. Maybe once in two or three years. Why, I thought you knew all about it." And he began to tell her how, because it never rained, the Egyptians had dug ditches from the river out across the valley. They dug other ditches from these, and still others from these until all the green valley of Egypt was crisscrossed with ditches. Into them the slaves dipped buckets fastened to long poles, which they called *shadufs*, and then poured the water on the fields.

"But doesn't the water in the river ever give out?" asked Sari.

"No," answered Kaffe. "Never, because once every year Osiris, god of the Nile, sends a flood. The river gets bigger and bigger and runs out into all the ditches until they are full of water, and when they can't hold any more it floods the land too. Then, after a while, the water goes

61

down again and leaves the ground moist and ready for planting, with a fine new covering of rich soil that Osiris sent down with the flood."

"Shall we see the flood?" cried Sari. "When does it come?"

"Of course we'll see it," said Kaffe. "It covers everything except the villages and houses. It can't reach them because they are built on high land. And it will be here any day now. It always comes at this time of the year. That is why nobody started planting after the harvest."

"Well!" said Sari. "This certainly is a strange country."

"Why?" asked Kaffe.

"Because here you stay in one place and wait for the river to come and grow your food for you. In my country, when the sheep and goats have eaten up all the grass, we move on until we find more grass that is all grown for us."

"But how can you move your house and your furniture around all the time?"

"We don't have much furniture, and our houses are made of skins so that they can be folded up and carried around."

62

"And you say Egypt is a strange country!" Kaffe laughed. "That's the strangest thing I ever heard of."

"It's not a bit stranger than your flood. Do you think that if we sit here for a while and watch, we can see it coming?"

"We might," said Kaffe. "But it may not come until tomorrow or the next day, or next week, and that would be an awfully long time to sit and watch. Let's think of something else to do."

"We could play ball," said Sari.

"We played that yesterday."

"We might get the draught board and play Jackals and Hounds."

"Oh, that's too hard work," objected Kaffe. (Jackals and Hounds was a game something like chess.)

"Then you think of something," said Sari.

Kaffe closed his eyes and thought. He thought so hard that he wrinkled his forehead, but that didn't seem to help. He had almost given up when suddenly he did think of something.

"I know," he cried. "Let's play we are Sand People like you, and that the grass has given out and we have to move to another place to find some more. We can take

63

our lunch and then come back here and pretend that this is a new place."

Sari clapped her hands. "Let's," she said.

"Go to the kitchen and tell Cook to put up some lunch for us, and I'll tell Mother what we are going to do," ordered Kaffe as they started downstairs.

Kaffe could not find Nasha anywhere in the house. One of her women said that she had gone to the slave quarters. Kaffe thought of going to find her, but then he remembered that if he and Sari had to go off in search of grass, they would have to hurry. He decided to tell his father instead. He found Socharis sitting in his great carved chair reading a papyrus scroll. He seemed to be very much interested in what it said, for when Kaffe spoke to him, he only grunted.

"Father, Sari and I are going on a picnic. We're going to pretend that we are Sand People looking for new grass," explained Kaffe.

"Ummm," said Socharis, without looking up from his reading. Kaffe wondered whether his father had really heard what he said. He almost said it again, but then he thought that Socharis might not want to be bothered, so he said good-bye and tiptoed out of the room.

Sari met him at the kitchen door carrying a reed basket. Together they set off toward the gate which opened on the road.

Ani waved to them as they passed the field where he was raking up stubble. "Where are you going?" he asked.

"We're Sand People, and we are moving to another place where there will be more grass for our cattle," Kaffe answered. He was already pretending very hard.

"Oh, I see," said Ani. "I wish you good fortune."

The children waved good-bye to him and went through the gate into the road.

"Where shall we go?" asked Kaffe then.

"I don't know," answered Sari. "The men always decided where we were to go next, so you will have to do it."

"We might go out to the desert. There's sand there, so that ought to be a good place for Sand People to go."

"We didn't live where there was just sand. There had to be grass, too," Sari reminded him. "Mostly we stayed on the edge of the desert."

"This desert has an edge," pointed out Kaffe. "You

65

can see it off there. That's where those yellow cliffs are."

"Let's go there, then," said Sari.

They started up the road, but they had not walked very far before Kaffe said, "This road won't lead us to the desert. It goes to the temple, and then on to Memphis. I think the shortest way would be to go across the fields. It isn't very far that way." The yellow cliffs beyond the level green valley did look very near.

The road, which was really a dike on which people could travel across the country at flood time, was high above the fields, so the children scrambled down the bank, splashed through the ditch at the bottom, and climbed up into the field beyond.

At first they had a wonderful time. They herded their cattle and kept them headed toward the cliffs as good shepherds should. When one strayed off, they rounded it up and brought it back. They talked about all the things that are important to Sand People, and once they even had a fight with another tribe which tried to take their herds away from them. They talked about how much they needed new grass, and how much longer they could go on without finding a water hole. And all the time they were making their way steadily westward, across the fields and over the ditches, toward the desert.

The sun climbed higher and higher overhead and got hotter and hotter. Kaffe and Sari began to get very hungry, and soon they found a large fig tree with a broad patch of shade beneath it, and sat down to eat their lunch. Sari took a jar of milk from the basket, and some wheat cakes and radishes and little green onions and figs. They finished everything and threw the crumbs on the ground for the birds. Then, because the sun was so hot and because they had eaten so much, they began to feel sleepy. "We might pretend that it is night, now, and that we are going to sleep," said Kaffe, yawning.

"All right," agreed Sari. "Do you think we ought to tether the cattle?"

"I don't think they will wander away," answered Kaffe. "Let's just leave—them—as—they—are——" With that he was sound asleep.

It was the middle of the afternoon when they awoke, and the sun was already sliding downhill toward the west.

"We shouldn't have slept so long," said Kaffe. "We'll have to hurry if we want to get there and home again before supper."

They picked up their basket and started on again. They walked and walked, but they soon began to notice that the yellow cliffs seemed almost as far away as they had when they started out that morning.

"Sari," said Kaffe finally, "the desert is farther away than I thought it was."

Sari did not answer. They walked on.

Then Kaffe said, "Perhaps we had better go back. After all, we can pretend that we got there—and we can come again some other day when we can start earlier," he added quickly.

Sari looked back over her shoulder the way they had come. The fields stretched far behind them. She couldn't even see the temple road or the villa.

"I think we had better go back," she said. "They might worry about us if we were gone too long. Besides, we haven't any more food."

So they turned back. They walked and they walked, and they did not stop now to herd their cattle. In fact, they had forgotten all about them. All they wanted was to get home, and home was a long way off.

"I didn't think we had come so far," said Kaffe at last.

"Neither did I," said Sari in a small voice. "My feet hurt," she added.

"So do mine," said Kaffe.

They walked on across more fields and splashed through more ditches. Finally they came to one where the water was halfway to their knees.

"I don't remember crossing as deep a ditch as this, do you?" asked Sari as they climbed the bank on the other side.

"No, but we must have," said Kaffe. "I remember those three palm trees over there, and besides, here are our footprints pointing the other way."

They crossed the field and came to the next ditch. Here, too, the water was much deeper than they remembered it. Suddenly Kaffe realized what was happening.

"Sari!" he cried in a frightened voice. "I know why the water is deeper. It's the flood. Come on! We'll have to hurry."

They began to run over the uneven ground. In each ditch they came to the water was deeper than it had been in the one before it. First it came to their knees, then

69

to the edge of their kilts. Then they began getting wet in earnest.

The water was muddy, too. Kaffe and Sari looked more and more bedraggled as they hurried on. To make matters worse, the sun at last sank behind the desert cliffs and it began to get dark. Sari began to whimper a little.

"Don't worry," said Kaffe, trying to comfort her. "I can see the temple road." He pointed ahead to where the dike stood up like a ridge in the twilight.

They began to run, but they were very tired and it was hard going over the muddy ground.

"There! We're almost home," said Kaffe cheerfully. "Only one more field. Then we can climb up on the dike and we'll be there."

He stepped down into the ditch that separated them from the field. He went down and down, and began to be frightened, for he could not reach the bottom of the ditch. At last, when he touched bottom, the water was up to his armpits. He held out his hand to Sari. She was scared, too, for the water was up to her chin. Half swimming, half walking, Kaffe struggled to the other side of the ditch, pulling Sari after him. Then they clambered

70

up the bank and started across the last field, shivering in the cool evening air.

They wasted no time in talking, but ran as fast as they could toward the dike. Kaffe sighed with relief as they reached the last ditch. On the other side of it was the sloping wall of the dike. Then his heart sank right down into his wet bare feet, for what he saw in front of him was not a ditch any longer. It was a river. It was only then that he remembered that this was one of the main ditches, bigger than the rest, which fed all the small ditches they had been crossing.

"Look, Sari," was all that he could say. They were so discouraged that they sat right down on the muddy bank and didn't say another word. They were wet and cold and hungry and very much frightened.

Sari began to cry. Kaffe wanted to cry himself, but he swallowed the lump in his throat and said to Sari, "Crying won't do any good. There's enough water here already. Come on! Let's shout. Someone will surely hear us."

So Sari stopped crying and they both shouted, but everybody was snugly at home that night and there was no one around to hear them.

After a while they stopped, and Kaffe said, "They'll surely miss us at home before long. I told Father what we were going to do." Then he remembered that he had wondered, when he spoke to Socharis, if his father had heard what he said, and he did not feel at all sure, sitting there on the wet bank, that Socharis had. But he did not tell Sari. They just sat there, saying nothing, and waited for someone to find them.

Meanwhile, back at the villa, Nasha was saying to Socharis, "Where are Kaffe and Sari? They must have had their supper at Sari's house, but it seems to me that they ought to be back by this time. It's dark."

"Oh, they'll be along," said Socharis absent-mindedly.

But they did not come along, and finally Nasha said, "I'm going to send Num after them. I don't like to have them wandering around in the dark on a night like this. They might fall into a ditch and be drowned."

So Num was sent running down to the little mud-brick house where Sari and Ben and Neemat lived. When he asked for the children, Neemat said, "Why, no. They aren't here. I thought they were at the villa. I haven't seen them all day."

She and Ben followed Num back to the villa. When Nasha heard that the children had not been at Sari's house and that no one had seen them since morning, she became very much frightened.

Then Socharis remembered something. "It seems to me," he said, "that Kaffe came in this morning and said that he and Sari were going off somewhere . . . but I was reading and I don't remember where."

"Oh, Socharis," said Nasha, "you must remember. They may have got caught in the flood if they went far."

"Someone must have seen them go," said Socharis. "Num, go and ask the other slaves."

By the time Num had asked about the children and had found that Ani had seen them turn into the temple road, everyone was very concerned indeed, and Nasha and Neemat were crying. Socharis was as alarmed as the rest, but he gave his orders calmly. Everyone was so eager to start hunting for the missing children that almost before you could count ten there was a long line of slaves in front of the villa with torches in their hands. Socharis took a torch, too, and he was so worried about the children that he forgot that Egyptian nobles never walked around the countryside. Probably he did not

73

even remember that he owned a litter. Anyway, he started off on foot at the head of the procession.

Just about the time they were first missed at home, the water began to lap around the children's feet. They moved farther away from the bank, but the water seemed to be playing tag with them. It came right after them. Kaffe really began to be afraid then. "Suppose nobody finds us and the water keeps on getting higher and higher," he thought. He looked around but there was not even a tree that they could climb. He forgot that he was almost grown up and began to cry, and Sari, seeing his tears, started to cry, too.

Just then Kaffe heard a faint sound in the distance, as if someone were coming along the dike. He listened, holding his breath. The sound became louder. It was —it was—footsteps!

"Sari," he cried, "I hear someone coming."

Sari heard the footsteps then, too.

"Come on! Shout, so that they'll know we are here," cried Kaffe. They shouted at the top of their lungs and kept on shouting. They hardly dared stop to draw breath for fear they would not be heard.

Soon they could see a dark shape coming along the dike. As it came nearer, they saw that it was a litter, carried by slaves. There was someone seated in it. They shouted again, just as loud as they could, but the swiftly running water in the ditch was making a great deal of noise, so that at first they thought no one was going to hear them. Then, when they had almost given up hope, they heard a man's voice say, "Hark! Did you hear someone shouting?"

The voice sounded familiar. The litter stopped and the children shouted again.

"Who is there?" called the voice.

"Oserkaf, a son of Socharis, and his slave, Sari," Kaffe called back. "We are caught by the flood. We can't get across the ditch."

They could see the litter being slowly lowered to the ground. The man who had called to them got out.

"Kaffe and Sari?" asked the voice. "What are you doing here so far from home?" The voice did not sound pleased to find them there, but Kaffe didn't care, for he knew now who the man was.

"Anhotep!" he cried, and he was so glad to see someone who could help them that he forgot that he had no

75

love for Anhotep. He even forgot that the Nubian had gashed Red Boy's chest.

A great deal happened very quickly after that. Anhotep's tallest slave made his way down the bank and across the ditch. He took Kaffe on his shoulders and carried him through the water to the wall of the dike. Then he went back for Sari. It seemed no time at all before both children were standing safe and sound on the temple road.

Anhotep made room for them on a chest that he was carrying in his litter. It was a rather hard and joggly seat, but it seemed to the children to be the most comfortable place in the world after the long time they had spent in the wet field. They sat there at Anhotep's feet, and while the slaves made their way down the temple road toward the villa, they told him their story. By the time they had finished they had reached their own gate.

There, to Kaffe's surprise, Anhotep ordered the litter to be set down. "I hope that you will pardon me if I leave you here instead of taking you to your door," he said politely. "But I am still a long way from home, and the flood is rising so fast that I am afraid I shall have the same trouble you had if I do not hurry. Besides," he added, "I see men with torches coming to look for you."

The procession of slaves, led by Socharis, was indeed nearing the gate. When the children saw it, they quickly said good-bye to Anhotep and, tired as they were, ran up the road to meet the searchers. They were so eager to tell everybody they were safe that they did not notice how hurriedly Anhotep's litter moved down the road.

After that, they were soon back at the villa. Everyone was so glad to see them that nobody even scolded them for going so far away.

When they were clean and dry and warm once more, Num brought in their supper, and while they ate, Socharis, Nasha, Ben and Neemat listened to their story. After they had finished telling their adventures (and had told some of them two or three times), Nasha took Kaffe to his room. Ben picked up Sari in his arms, and he and Neemat went back to their little house beyond the garden wall. Sari was asleep before they reached home, and Kaffe was asleep almost before Nasha had left his bedside. But Socharis and Nasha stayed up long afterward talking it all over.

"If Anhotep had not come along just when he did," said Nasha at last, "they might have been drowned."

"Yes. It is lucky for us that he was on that road just then. I must write to him and thank him for doing us so great a service," said Socharis. He thought for a moment. Then he said, "But doesn't it seem strange to you, Nasha, that he left the children at our gate and went off without waiting to speak to me?"

"He told Kaffe that he was afraid of being caught by the flood before he could get home," Nasha reminded him.

"I don't understand why," said Socharis. "He can follow the dike all the way to his own gate, just as we can here. Besides, it seems queer to me that any man would be traveling around the country on the first night of the flood."

"Oh, Socharis," said Nasha. "Probably he didn't know the flood was coming any more than the children did. I think you are very suspicious. We can never be grateful enough to him for rescuing the children. What he happened to be doing is his own affair."

"Ummm," said Socharis. "I suppose you are right." But from the way he said it, Nasha knew that he was not satisfied.

6

At Gizeh

Very early one morning not long after the flood began,
Kaffe ran down the path from the villa to the house
where Sari lived. "Sari," he called as he ran into the
courtyard, "Sari, where are you?"

"Here I am," said Sari, coming out of the house. "What's the matter?"

Kaffe had run so fast that he was out of breath. "Father is going to Gizeh, and he says that we may go with him," he panted. "Come on! We are going to start right away."

When the two children reached the villa, Socharis was just settling himself in the litter. They climbed in beside him. Nasha was standing in the doorway waiting to wave good-bye to them.

"Can't you come, too, Mother?" asked Kaffe.

"Not today," answered Nasha. "I have too much to do here. You will have to remember everything you see, and tell me all about it when you get home—and," she added, "take care not to wander off and get lost again. I've had enough worry over you two lately."

"We won't," promised the children, and with that the slaves lifted the litter to their shoulders and set off quickly toward the gate and the temple road.

They passed the field where they had so nearly got caught in the flood. There was no field there now, for it was all under water. From the dike it looked as though the whole world was flooded. Villas and villages rose above the water like islands, and dikes stood up like ridges, but everything else was covered with reddish-brown water right up to the edge of the yellow cliffs that Kaffe and Sari had tried so hard to reach on the day that they had pretended they were Sand People.

Sari looked out over the valley as the slaves carried them swiftly along past the temple and out on the road to Memphis. "Egypt is very flat, isn't it?" she asked Kaffe.

"I don't know. Is it?" said Kaffe.

"Yes. In our country there were mountains in some places, and the land was all hilly and uneven."

"What are mountains?" asked Kaffe.

"Why, great high piles of rock that go up and up to points against the sky."

"Oh, I know," said Kaffe. "We have them, too, only we call them pyramids. The pharaohs build them for their tombs."

"Nobody builds mountains," said Sari. "They are just there."

"How could they be?" began Kaffe, but Socharis interrupted him.

"Sari is right, Kaffe," he said. "There are mountains in her country, and they are not pyramids. They are like the cliffs there at the edge of the desert, only much higher. The copper that we use comes from some of them."

"Oh," said Kaffe. "Well, anyway, a pyramid is something like a mountain, isn't it?"

"Well, something like it," admitted Socharis.

"You'll see one when we get to Gizeh," Kaffe told Sari.

Socharis pointed out over the flooded fields. "You can see it right now," he said, and there, far off on the edge of the desert to the north, was the tip of the pyramid that Khufu, the Pharaoh of Egypt, was building.

"Does it look like a mountain, Sari?" asked Kaffe eagerly.

"Not very much, from here," answered Sari. Then, seeing that Kaffe was disappointed, she said, "But maybe it will when we get closer to it."

"It does look pretty small now," said Kaffe.

"It is because it is so large that we can see it from way off here," said Socharis. "No pharaoh has ever built a pyramid as big as the one that Khufu is building."

"It has taken a long time to build it, hasn't it, Father?" asked Kaffe.

"Yes, indeed. Almost sixteen years, with a hundred thousand men working on it every year at flood time, and it is not finished yet," answered Socharis.

"But why do they work on it just at flood time?" asked Kaffe.

"Because it is easier to float the stone across the river from the quarries when the land is flooded," answered Socharis. "And besides, the slaves are needed for farming the rest of the year."

"That's right," said Kaffe. "I forgot. Some of our slaves went to Gizeh last week to work on the pyramid, didn't they?"

"Yes, Khufu ordered me to send them," said Socharis. Even noblemen's slaves were drafted for work on the pyramid if Khufu needed them.

The litter jogged on and on along the dike, through the city of Memphis, then out on the dike again. They began to pass groups of slaves, like those from their own farm, going to work on the pyramid. They saw others who were staggering toward Memphis with bandaged arms or legs or bloody backs, worn out and injured from

83

helping to heave the heavy blocks of stone into place. But all of them, tired and ill, or well and strong, bowed to the earth as Socharis' litter passed them.

Now the children could see the pyramid rising high above the yellow desert. Its top was smooth and finished but the lower part was black with workmen.

Soon they entered the new city that Khufu had built near his tomb. It was almost as large as Memphis. The streets were alive with people hurrying to and fro as though what they were doing was very important.

They passed the shining new palace and unpainted mud-brick houses where the workmen lived. Then they went on, out into the country again, toward the sandy desert and the great pyramid. It loomed higher and higher above them until at last Sari said, almost in a whisper, "It does look like a mountain, Kaffe. A great, steep mountain that no one could ever climb."

But Kaffe did not answer. He was too busy looking.

They rounded a corner of the pyramid and came to a standstill in front of its eastern side. Here the stone-work was finished almost to the bottom, and slaves were already laying the foundations for a T-shaped temple where, after the pharaoh's death, people would come to

They rounded a corner of the pyramid

worship his soul. This was what Socharis had come to see. Their slaves set down the litter and, followed by Num, Socharis walked over to the place where the temple was to be.

Kaffe and Sari stayed near the litter. No one paid any attention to them, but they were so busy watching the workmen that they did not mind. From the edge of the valley to the top of the desert cliff where the pyramid was being built ran a smooth stone runway. Up it struggled hundreds of slaves with ropes tied around their waists, dragging behind them a wooden sled loaded with great blocks of limestone. Every time the sled moved there was a grating, screeching sound. Mingled with that were the groans of the slaves, the shouts of the overseers and the crack of their whips on the slaves' bare backs.

The slaves working on the sides of the pyramid groaned, too, as they pushed the huge stone blocks into place. There were so many people and so much noise that it reminded Kaffe of bees swarming about some strange new kind of hive.

By the time Socharis came back, the children were almost dizzy from watching everything and from looking

86

up nearly five hundred feet to the top of the great stone pile. They were also bursting with questions.

"Father," cried Kaffe as soon as he saw Socharis, "where will they put Khufu's body when he dies? Does it go under the pyramid? How do they get it there?"

"No, not *under* it, *in* it," said Socharis, smiling. "It is hard to believe, isn't it, that there are passageways and rooms inside?"

"But how does anyone get in?" asked Kaffe. "I don't see a door anywhere."

"There is one, though," Socharis told him.

"Where?" asked both children.

"I don't know," answered Socharis. "That is a secret. Khufu doesn't want anybody to know where the door is, for someone might try to get in and steal his treasures. Someone might even try to steal the jewels from his body after he dies."

"But," exclaimed Kaffe, "that's a terrible thing to do, isn't it? To steal from the dead?"

"Indeed it is," answered Socharis, "but there are people who do it. We have all built false passageways and false doors in our tombs and have made the real ones hard to find so that tomb robbers can't get in. Would

87

you like to come with me now to see my tomb?" he added. "I want to find out how much the workmen have done."

He said this just as if he were inviting someone to come and see a house that he was building. And that is just what he was doing. Every Egyptian nobleman began to build his tomb when he was quite young, for he wanted to have a house all ready for his soul to live in when he died. Since his soul would have to live in this house for a much longer time than his body would live on earth, he was very careful to make the tomb beautiful, and to put into it everything that his soul would need to make it happy. There were bright pictures painted on the walls, and splendid furniture, and jars of food and wine, and jewelry and all sorts of treasures. Whatever anyone wanted to have with him after he died, he put into his tomb. The pharaoh had more things in his tomb than anybody else, but noblemen like Socharis had many treasures in theirs, too.

So Socharis and Kaffe and Sari got into the litter again and set out to see Socharis' tomb. Off in the desert near the pyramid, the children could see a great many little stone buildings built in rows, but they were not like pyra-

They stepped out of the litter at the door
and went inside

mids. They were flat topped, with sloping sides and a doorway in the middle of one wall. They were called mastabas. These were the tombs of the nobles, and the one that Socharis was building was quite close to the pyramid, which showed that Khufu liked him very much. No one could build his tomb at Gizeh unless Khufu told him he might, and only the people he liked best were allowed to build close to his pyramid.

They stepped out of the litter at the door and went inside. The workmen must have worked very hard, for the walls of the room were all smoothly plastered, and now a man was painting pictures on them. Across the room from the door was painted something that looked like another doorway. Above it was painted Re, the Sun God, with his bright wings, just as the children had seen him in the courtyard of the temple at home, and on either side of this strange door was painted a tall guard with a spear in his hand.

"Is that a real door?" asked Sari.

"No," answered Kaffe. "That is the door through which Father's soul will go to the world of the dead."

They began to walk around the room, looking at the

pictures. They were painted in strips on the walls, so there was room for a great many of them.

"Why," said Sari, "there is your father!" And there on the wall was a painting of Socharis in his big, carved chair, with a tiny slave kneeling before him.

"Why has the painter made your father so big and the slave so small?" asked Sari.

"Because Father is a very important person and the slave is not important at all," explained Kaffe.

"Oh," said Sari.

There were pictures of the villa, and pictures of slaves sowing and harvesting, of women working at their looms, and pictures of feasts, and pictures of hunts in the papyrus marshes. Pictures even of the animals—Nep and Sut and Red Boy among them. And there was still one whole wall not yet started. That gave Kaffe an idea. "Father," he called across the room to Socharis, "can't the painter put a picture of Sari and me on that wall?"

Socharis and the painter with whom he was talking smiled.

"Perhaps he could," said Socharis. "I have not decided what to put there. I shall have to think about it.

It is time, now, for us to go back to the city. We must have our lunch and I must see about the things that Khufu is having made for his pyramid."

"My!" said Kaffe as they got into the litter. "This has been an exciting morning." But he never guessed as he said it that the afternoon was going to be more exciting still.

7

The Green Stone

After lunch, Socharis, Kaffe and Sari set out for the part
of the new city where the craftsmen had their work-
shops. These men were making the treasures for Khufu's pyramid, and it was Socharis' job to see that every-

thing they made was just the way Khufu wanted it to be.

They left the litter in front of the cabinet-makers' shop. All the workmen bowed low before Socharis as he came in, and when he asked to see the chair that was being made for the chamber in the pyramid, the master cabinet-maker took them to the back of the shop. There, in the middle of the floor, stood a huge chair of carved ebony, inlaid with silver and gold and ivory.

Socharis looked it over carefully. "That is most satisfactory," he said. "Khufu will be pleased."

Next they went to the potter's, where they saw rows and rows of green and blue pottery jars and bowls in which some of the food for the pyramid was to be put. From there they walked on to the vasemaker's. Here, the workmen were busy working on the stone vases and jars for the pyramid. Some were small enough to hold in one's hand. Others were as long as a man's arm, and all of them were beautifully rounded and polished.

One man was working on a tall vase made of a white stone called alabaster. He had rubbed it with a stone polisher until it was so thin light shone through it. Beside him, another man was holding the vase he was mak-

94

ing between his knees. He gripped it with his feet while he turned a copper drill to shape it. Kaffe and Sari would like to have stayed there all afternoon watching the men work, but when Socharis had finished his business, he called them, and again they went out into the street.

This time they turned from the street through a gate into a large courtyard. Beyond this were other courtyards, and in all of them men were working with gold and silver and precious stones. This great place was the shop in which all the most precious jewelry was being made for the pyramid. In each courtyard the craftsmen were doing something different. Some were working with hammers and forges. Some were making gold beading. Others were pounding silver bars into wire, or covering carved gold with colored enamel.

Socharis inspected everything they were doing, and Kaffe and Sari looked over his shoulder, their eyes round with wonder at seeing so many beautiful things.

But at last Socharis was finished with Khufu's business. "Now," he said briskly, "just one more thing, and then we can start for home."

"What is that?" asked Kaffe.

"I am having a pair of silver bracelets made for your mother," said Socharis. "I want to go and pick out the stones with which they are to be set."

"Silver bracelets?" asked Kaffe. "How wonderful!" And indeed they were, for silver in Egypt was more precious than gold because there was less of it. There were few men who could give their wives silver bracelets for a gift.

They came out into the sunny street again. "There is a lapidary who has a shop in this street," said Socharis. "We shall go there."

"What is a lapidary?" asked Kaffe. He had never heard the word before.

"A man who cuts and polishes precious stones," answered Socharis.

They found the shop and went in. It was a tiny shop, almost like the one in which Kaffe had bought Sari's doll that day in Memphis.

"What kind of stones are you going to get?" asked Kaffe.

"Turquoises," said Socharis. "Let me see some," he said to the shopkeeper.

Socharis sat down at a table in the middle of the shop.

The jeweler brought out a little leather bag from which he poured a heap of bright blue turquoises. They were a lovely color, but Socharis took so long in choosing the ones he wanted that Kaffe and Sari, tired of watching him, began to look around the shop.

There was not a great deal to see except some big lumps of uncut stone. Some of it was dark blue. That was lapis lazuli. There were pieces of reddish-brown carnelian, too, and green malachite. After they had looked at these, the children went over to the lapidary's workbench and looked at his tools, but that was not very interesting. They were just going back to watch Socharis again, when Sari stubbed her toe against a basket under the workbench and tipped it over. Out of it rolled chips of stone and all sorts of odds and ends. Sari got down on her knees and gathered them up again.

"There! Have I got them all now? Oh, no—here's another piece. Why, what is it?" she asked, looking at the little piece of stone she held in her hand.

"Let's see," said Kaffe. He took the little piece of green stone. It was oval in shape, about an inch long, and on its smoothly polished surface was carved the figure of a hawk, unmistakable with its curved beak.

"Why, that is Horus, the son of Osiris, the god of the Nile," exclaimed Kaffe in surprise. "Let's show it to my father."

They went back to the table where Socharis was still poring over the turquoises. "See what we found," said Kaffe.

He dropped the little green stone into his father's hand.

"Very nice carving, Master," said the lapidary, "only it is chipped." He pointed to a little nick in one edge.

But Socharis was not listening. He was turning the stone over and over, looking at it very carefully. "Where did you get this?" he asked the lapidary at last. Kaffe could tell by the sound of his father's voice that he was very angry.

"A man came in the other day," answered the lapidary. "He said his master wanted to sell it——"

Socharis stood up. "No, no! Tell me the truth," he commanded.

The lapidary was frightened. He wrung his hands. "It is the truth, Master," he cried. "I bought it as I said. Some other old jewelry, too. The stones, I kept. The gold settings I sold to the goldsmiths to melt up and use again."

"But the stone is chipped," said Socharis. "You could not hope to sell it."

"No, Master, but it is a very fine carving. I thought I might try to make one like it sometime."

Socharis said nothing. He seemed to be thinking hard. Then, "Let me see the other stones you bought," he said.

The man disappeared into a little room behind the shop. He returned with a small box which he put into Socharis' hands. In it were many fine pieces of carnelian and turquoise and lapis lazuli. They looked as if they had once been set in a jeweled collar, or perhaps in bracelets and rings.

"You have already sold the settings to the goldsmiths?" asked Socharis sharply.

"Yes, Master. Last week."

"Then there is no use in looking for them," said Socharis. "They will have been melted down by this time. Would you know the man who sold you the jewels if you should see him again?" he added.

The lapidary was not sure. "He was only a slave," he

explained, "or perhaps an overseer. But his master must have been a noble like yourself, Master, to own such jewels."

"That is it exactly," said Socharis. "I do not believe he owned them, whoever he was."

The lapidary went pale. "You mean, Master . . ."

"I mean," said Socharis clearly, "that I think these jewels, or at least this stone, have been stolen—stolen from the pyramid of Sneferu, the father of Khufu."

The poor lapidary sank on his knees. He was trembling. "Mercy, oh, mercy, Master," he wailed. "I did not know it. I swear!"

Kaffe and Sari were nearly bursting with excitement. "How do you know, Father? Tell us," begged Kaffe.

But Socharis did not answer his question. Instead he said to the lapidary, "I think you have told me the truth. If you have, you need not fear, for Khufu is just. He must be told of this, however. I myself shall take the stone to him and tell him your story. Come, children," he added. "We must go at once to the palace."

It was not until they were back in the litter hurrying toward the palace as fast as the slaves could go that Kaffe dared say any more to his father. Socharis sat very straight beside him, frowning. He looked very stern. But at last Kaffe asked, "Did the stone belong to Sneferu, Father?"

"I think so," said Socharis.

"How can you tell?" asked Kaffe.

"It was the chip in it, wasn't it, Master?" asked Sari shyly.

Socharis smiled. "That was one thing that told me," he answered. "But now you will have to be patient and not ask any more questions. You will soon know all about it." They had come to the palace gates.

Beyond the gates was a wide square with statues of the pharaoh set around it, and in the farther wall, a double doorway with one entrance painted white, the other red. Through this the slaves carried the litter into a courtyard and across it to the inner door of the palace. There the litter was set down, and Socharis and the children got out. The palace door was guarded by two tall Nubians, their spears crossed to keep out anybody who had no business to enter. But as soon as they saw Socharis, they lowered their spears and let him and the two children pass.

In the hall of the palace they were met by other

guards, and to one of these Socharis said, "Tell your master, Khufu, that Socharis has come to see him on a matter of the greatest importance."

The slave ran off, and the visitors waited for him to deliver the message to Khufu. The room in which they stood was more beautiful than any the children had ever seen, but they were too excited to pay much attention to it. It seemed at least an hour before the guard came back to say that Khufu would see them, and led them through the palace into the garden.

There in a great carved chair inlaid with gold and silver sat Khufu, the Pharaoh of Egypt, surrounded by his slaves, who were singing and playing on flutes and harps to entertain him. He was a tall man with an arched nose and piercing dark eyes. He wore a high red crown on his head, a wide gold collar around his neck, and a white linen kilt as fine as silk.

When he saw the pharaoh, Socharis walked slowly toward him, bowing as he went. Kaffe did just as his father did, and Sari, being only a slave, knelt and touched her head to the ground as Socharis had told her she must.

Khufu rose from his chair and came to meet Socharis. After they had greeted each other, he said, "Your news must indeed be important, Socharis, to bring you so unexpectedly to see me."

"It is," answered Socharis. "In fact, it is so important that I beg you to send your slaves away while I tell it to you."

Khufu was very much surprised at that, but since he trusted Socharis, he did as his visitor asked.

While the slaves were picking up their instruments and bringing a chair for Socharis, Khufu said to him, "Who are these children with you? Why, surely this one cannot be Kaffe! What a great boy he has become!" He smiled down at Kaffe, who felt very much pleased that Khufu remembered him after such a long time. The pharoah had not seen Kaffe since he was five or six.

"And the little girl, who is she?" asked Khufu.

"If you please, sir, that is my slave, Sari," said Kaffe.

"And is she to stay while I send my slaves away?" Khufu asked jokingly.

"As you wish, sir," answered Kaffe politely, "but she is the one who found what Father has come to show you."

"Then we shall have to let her stay," said Khufu, and he smiled at Sari, too. "Now, Socharis," he said, "what is this that you have come to tell me?"

But Socharis did not tell him at once. Instead he said, "Do you remember, Khufu, that when we were boys—though I was by far the younger—we used to have our lessons together in the palace at Memphis? And that often, after we had finished our studying, your father, the great Sneferu, would romp with us in the garden and ask us about what we had learned?"

Khufu looked puzzled. "Of course I remember," he said.

Socharis went on. "And do you remember," he said, "the day that Uni, the stone carver, came with the stone that he had carved with the figure of the great God Horus, which was to be set in a ring for your father?"

Khufu smiled. "Well do I remember that," he said, "for it was I who dropped the stone and chipped it. I thought surely I would be punished, but my father was a fair man. He saw that it was an accident, and told Uni that he would keep the stone even though it was chipped, because by that mark he would always be able to recognize it as his own."

"Was the ring with that stone in it buried with him when he died?" asked Socharis.

"Yes," answered Khufu. "I myself saw that it was done."

"Good," said Socharis. He pulled the stone from his girdle where he had hidden it. "Is this that stone?" he asked.

Khufu started. He looked at the little carved stone lying in the palm of Socharis' hand as if he could not believe his eyes. Kaffe and Sari saw his face slowly redden with anger. He took the stone and looked at it. At last he said, "There is no doubt about it, Socharis. This belonged to my father. Where did you find it?"

Socharis told him the story of finding the stone. When he had finished, Khufu sat for a moment staring at the stone in his hand. Then he said, "Your finding this stone can mean only one thing. Someone has robbed my father's pyramid . . . But who, Socharis?" he asked. "Who would dare to do such a thing?"

Khufu sprang from his chair and began to stride angrily up and down the path. "We must find out who it is," he cried. "But how?"

"Perhaps——" began Socharis. Then he stopped. One

did not offer suggestions to the Pharaoh of Egypt unless he asked for them.

"What were you going to say, Socharis?" asked Khufu then. "If you have a plan, tell me what it is."

"You might send someone you can trust to the tomb to find out how much has been taken," suggested Socharis, "and whether there is anything left for which the robbers might return. If some of the treasure remains, you could set a trap for them."

"Good," said Khufu. "You yourself shall go to the pyramid, Socharis, for I know that I can trust you."

"You wish me to go at once?" asked Socharis.

"Yes. Tonight after dark. You can use your own litter and everyone will think that you are going home. Tomorrow morning, when you return, no one will think anything about it—except, perhaps, that you are doing a great deal of business here at the palace. We must keep this a secret if we are to catch the robbers."

Socharis bowed his head. "It shall be done, Khufu," he said, "but give me leave to do one thing before I go."

"What is that?" asked Khufu.

"To send my slave, Num, home with these two children."

"Send them home?" asked Khufu. "For what reason? Send a message to Nasha telling her that you are all staying here for the night. It is time Kaffe came to know my sons. They will have need of him when he grows up, as I have need of you. Better that they should learn to be friends now than wait till later."

So it was arranged. And while Socharis sent Num home with the message for Nasha, Kaffe and Sari were led off to meet the pharaoh's children.

8
Sneferu's Pyramid

All the rest of the afternoon, Kaffe and Sari had a wonderful time playing with the royal children in the palace
garden. Khufu was older than Socharis, so most of his
children were older than Kaffe, but there was one boy

of ten, and another boy and girl who were not much
older. The three of them and Kaffe and Sari had such
a good time playing games and splashing in the garden
pool that by bedtime they all felt very well ac-
quainted.

At last they were sent to bed—or rather, Kaffe was.
Sari lay down on a mat at the foot of his bed. But neither
of them went to sleep. They were much too excited to be
sleepy, so they lay and watched the darkness fall over
the garden outside, and thought about the stone they
had found, and Socharis, who would soon be on his way
to Sneferu's pyramid.

"I wish we could go," said Kaffe wistfully.

Sari was thinking the same thing. "I wish we could,
too," she said.

They began to feel very sorry for themselves because
they were being left behind.

Then, suddenly, Kaffe sat up in bed. "Sari," he cried,
"we could go!"

Sari sat up, too. "How?" she asked.

"The litter is down in the courtyard," said Kaffe. "We
could hide under the cushions until they got started."

"But your father would send us back when he found us," said Sari.

"He couldn't," said Kaffe, "because he wouldn't have anybody to send back with us. Num has gone home and nobody else is going with Father except the slaves who carry the litter."

"But he would be very angry," said Sari.

Kaffe jumped out of bed and began to put on his kilt and sandals. "Yes, he would be, but he couldn't do anything except punish us. Just think," he went on, "how exciting it would be to ride out into the desert at night to a tomb that has been robbed. Why, we might even meet the robbers and have a fight! We couldn't miss anything like that. We must go. Come on! It's almost dark now. They'll be starting soon."

It took Sari only a minute to get ready. They crept out into the hall. "Do you know the way to the courtyard?" Sari whispered. "This is such a big place. We might get lost in it."

But they did not get lost, and no one saw them as they tiptoed to the courtyard door. The guards in the palace hall were probably eating their supper, for they were nowhere to be seen, but outside the door the children could hear the two Nubians talking. Kaffe had forgotten them.

"We can't get past them," whispered Sari.

"Not unless we can get them to go away for a minute," Kaffe whispered back.

"How can we?" asked Sari.

They crept right up to the door behind the guards. Then Kaffe leaned down and unstrapped one of his sandals. Sari watched him. He waited until both guards were looking the other way, then threw the sandal as hard as he could out into the courtyard. It fell with a soft plop on the brick pavement.

"What was that?" asked one guard.

"I didn't hear anything," said the other.

"I did," said the first one. "Come! We had better look around to be sure no one is hiding out there in the shadows."

They both moved away from the door, and as soon as they did, the two children crept out of the doorway and dashed to the nearest pillar. The guards did not hear them, and as they reached their hiding place, they heard one of the Nubians say, "This must be what made the noise. It's a sandal. Probably those willful children

111

of our master's are playing again after they are supposed to be in bed."

Kaffe and Sari sighed with relief. They crept carefully along from pillar to pillar until they reached the litter, then buried themselves under the cushions at the end where Socharis would put his feet. It was very hot and stuffy, but they had not been there more than a moment or two before they heard voices in the courtyard. The slaves were coming out to the litter.

The slaves stood talking among themselves while they waited for Socharis. Kaffe soon could tell by their voices that these were not the slaves who usually carried Socharis' litter. Suddenly there were more footsteps, and he heard his father say, "Ready, guards?"

"So," thought Kaffe, "these aren't just litter bearers whom Khufu has given us. They are real guards. This is going to be even more exciting than I had thought!"

The litter shook as Socharis got in and settled himself. One of his feet touched Kaffe's leg under the cushions, but if Socharis thought that the cushion had suddenly become hard and lumpy, he did not say anything. Probably he was busy thinking about the robbery of Sneferu's tomb and did not notice.

The slaves swung the litter to their shoulders and off they started toward the palace gates. Kaffe and Sari, of course, could not see anything, but they could tell pretty well where they were by the sounds they heard. They heard the guards challenge Socharis at the palace gates, and they heard the street noises as they went through the city. Then everything was quiet again and all they could hear was the padding sound of the slaves' feet on hard earth.

"We are on the dike," thought Kaffe to himself. "We ought to get to Memphis soon."

But the minutes went by—or maybe it was hours—and still they did not come to Memphis. It was a long time before Kaffe realized that they were not going to Memphis at all, but were taking another road which would lead them to the edge of the desert near Sneferu's pyramid. Kaffe had often seen this road far off across the valley, but he had never been on it.

By this time it seemed at least a hundred years since they had left the palace, and Kaffe began to wonder if the trip was going to be as much fun as he had imagined. Every part of him seemed to be asleep. There were pins and needles in his hands and feet, and he was nearly smothered. There was a feather from one of the pillows tickling his nose, too. That made him even more uncomfortable. Besides, he began to wonder just how he would tell Socharis that he and Sari were there, and when he would do it. Somehow the punishment that he was certainly going to get seemed more distasteful now than it had back in the bedroom at the palace.

But he didn't have to worry about it very long, because his fate was decided for him. It was the feather that did it. It kept right on tickling Kaffe's nose. Suddenly he knew he was going to sneeze, and there was nothing he could do to stop it. He tried to hold it back, but he couldn't, and so it was that Socharis heard a very loud "Kerchoo" from right under the cushions at his feet.

It did not take Socharis long to decide what to do. He ordered the litter set down, sprang out quickly and, seizing the cushions, threw them on the ground. Then he took hold of the children and pulled them out just the way he had the cushions. When he saw who they were, he was so astonished that all he could think of to say was, "*Where* did you come from?" He didn't sound at all happy to see them.

Kaffe and Sari were stiff from lying curled up under

the cushions, and the way Socharis was looking at them did not make them feel any better.

"From the palace," said Kaffe in a very small voice, answering Socharis' question. "We wanted to see Sneferu's pyramid," he added. But somehow, out there on the dike in the dead of night, with his father and the guards all staring at him and Sari, it did not sound like a very good reason for coming.

"And, I suppose," said Socharis, "you knew that when I discovered you were here, I could not send you back because I need all these men to carry the litter."

"Yes, Father," said Kaffe miserably. Then he added, "Won't you please punish us now and get it over with? It would be so much pleasanter."

"I have no doubt that it would," answered Socharis, "but I haven't time now. You can be certain, however, that I shall attend to it the first thing in the morning. Now get into the litter, and see that you do not cause any more trouble."

The guards had by this time put the cushions back where they belonged. Socharis stepped in, and the two children scrambled in after him. Away they went again toward the desert.

For a long time nobody said anything. The two children thought that perhaps the less they said, the better off they would be. Besides, it was so quiet that after a while they began to get sleepy. Pretty soon, in spite of all they could do, their heads nodded, and they fell asleep on each other's shoulders.

Some time later Kaffe woke up. The litter was doing very strange things. It was bobbing around like a ship in a storm. When he looked out from under the canopy, Kaffe saw why. They had left the valley behind them, and now all around them was the desert, dull and gray in the starlight. The bearers were plowing through the soft sand which gave under their feet and pitched the litter this way and that.

Kaffe nudged Sari. She woke up and saw where they were, too. They quite forgot that they were in disgrace, and Kaffe said to Socharis, "It's awfully dark out here, isn't it?" Somehow the wide, rolling desert didn't look like a very cozy place to spend the night.

"Yes, it is dark tonight," answered Socharis. "This is the night of the new moon, so there is no light to brighten the sand. But we are almost there now. See, there is the pyramid ahead of us. You can make it out against the sky if you look hard."

Kaffe and Sari strained their eyes through the darkness, and at last they saw it, too—another pyramid, smaller than Khufu's, but quite big enough to look very black and mysterious, rising up against the starry sky.

For no reason at all a shiver ran up Kaffe's spine and came down again. Sari, sitting close beside him, felt it.

"What's the matter?" she asked. "Are you cold?"

"No," said Kaffe. He would not admit that the dark night and the big pyramid looming up ahead of them made him feel suddenly afraid.

When they were quite near, Socharis ordered the litter to be set down behind a little hill of sand so that they were out of sight of the pyramid.

"Why do we stop here?" asked Kaffe in a whisper. He noticed that the guards were talking in whispers, too.

"There is no use in calling attention to ourselves in case anyone happens to be around, though I doubt if anyone is," answered Socharis. He called softly to the guards.

When they had gathered around, Socharis said

to them, "First we shall have to find out how the robbers got into the pyramid. That will probably take some time, as they may have covered up their tracks. Two men will stay here by the litter. The others will come with me. I shall shout if I need you," he added to the guards who were to stay by the litter.

"May Sari and I come with you?" asked Kaffe.

Socharis sighed. "I suppose you might as well," he said, "but you must stay with the guards. I am not going to finish this night by looking all over the desert for you, and you are not to go into the pyramid either with me or after me. Will you promise me that?"

"Yes," said both children, though Kaffe wanted dreadfully to go inside the pyramid, even if just the thought of it did scare him.

"Very well, then," said Socharis, and calling the guards, he and the children started off toward the pyramid.

When they reached it, Socharis turned to the guards. "I think it likely that the robbers tunneled in to one of the tomb passages, so let us search around the edge to see if we can find any traces of such a tunnel."

They worked along one side of the huge pile of stone then started along the next without seeing anything in the least out of the way. It was hard to see anything at all because it was so dark. Then one of the guards who had gone ahead gave a low cry. They ran up to him, and there, close to the side of the pyramid, was a large, dark hole like the entrance to a cave, with a sloping pathway leading down to it through the sand.

"Strange that they should leave it uncovered like that," said Socharis to one of the guards.

"Yes, Master, unless——"

"Unless what?" asked Socharis.

"Unless they were interrupted and had to leave suddenly. This entrance is on the desert side of the pyramid, and perhaps they thought it would not be noticed before they could get back and cover it up again."

"Very likely you are right," said Socharis. "Now light a torch for me. I am going inside."

"Alone, Master?" asked the guards.

"Yes," answered Socharis. "I do not think I shall need any help."

Kaffe thought the guards seemed relieved that they

did not have to go with Socharis, and he could not blame them. He thought his father was very brave to go into the tomb alone.

Socharis took the torch and made his way down the sloping path to the tunnel entrance. The children followed him. He flashed his torch inside, and they could see a narrow, steep passage that had been dug under the pyramid.

"Now," said Socharis, "you two stay right here until I come back. You are not to come one foot inside this passage. Do you understand?"

"Yes," said Kaffe. "We can't anyway. It will be too dark after you have taken the torch."

They stood there and watched Socharis start down the passage. His torch shone farther and farther away. Then it vanished, and they guessed that he had turned a corner. There was a dim glow for a second or two, and then that, too, faded away, and they were left staring into the dark hole in front of them.

It was rather frightening to wait there beside the black tunnel. The two children drew nearer together in the darkness. It was so still that they could hear the breathing of the guards who squatted at the head of the path to the tunnel. They could hear their own hearts beating, too, and not another sound. They looked up at the stars and off across the gray desert and wished that Socharis would hurry back with the torch.

They had been waiting for some time when Sari thought she saw something move just over the top of a little hill of sand near the pyramid. Her heart seemed to fly up into her mouth for a minute. She whispered to Kaffe, "Do you see anything moving over there?" She pointed to the sand hill.

Kaffe looked where she pointed. "No," he whispered back. "I don't see anything. Is it moving now?"

"No," said Sari, "it isn't, but I'm sure I saw something. It looked like a man's head."

They kept on watching, but everything was quiet, and the sand hill looked just the way a sand hill should. After a while Sari began to think she must have imagined seeing something bob up for a second against the sky.

Just the same, they did not feel very comfortable waiting there in the dark. It seemed hours since Socharis had left them. Finally, when they thought they could not bear it another minute, they heard a faint sound from inside the pyramid. A tiny, dull glow appeared at the back of the tunnel. Kaffe had just time to whisper to Sari, "Here comes Father," when they saw the light of a torch and heard the sound of running feet.

"Something must be the matter," said Kaffe. "He's running!"

Now they could see a figure holding a torch coming pell-mell toward them. Kaffe almost called out as he came nearer, but suddenly he held his breath. There was something unfamiliar about the figure racing toward them. Kaffe did not know what it was, but all at once he was sure that the man was not Socharis! And if it was not his father, it must be somebody who had no business there inside Sneferu's pyramid.

Kaffe did not have time after that to think what to do, for the man was almost at the tunnel entrance, so he went ahead and did the only thing he could to keep the stranger from getting away. He lowered his head, just as Red Boy did when he was charging in a fight, and hurled himself right at the stomach of the running man. There was the sound of someone falling heavily and then gasping for breath. Sari screamed, and Kaffe called to the guards for a torch.

He lowered his head, just as Red Boy did when he was charging in a fight

When the guards reached the tunnel, the light from the torch shone on such a strange scene that they cried out in surprise, for there was Kaffe sitting astride a man who was doubled up and groaning.

"Bring the torch nearer," cried Kaffe. "I want to see who he is."

The guards obeyed him. Then it was Kaffe's turn to cry out in amazement, for the man on the ground was none other than his old acquaintance, Anhotep!

For a moment Kaffe was terrified at what he had done. It was a serious matter to ram one's head into the stomach of an Egyptian noble and knock the breath out of him. But then a great many things began to flash through Kaffe's mind. He thought of the chest that Sari and he had sat on in Anhotep's litter on the night he rescued them from the flood, and how Anhotep left them at the gate and hurried away. He thought, too, of the bull that had cost a great deal of money, and of the stolen stone with the tiny hawk carved upon it.

"Sari," he cried, "I didn't make a mistake. Anhotep is the man who robbed the pyramid!"

By this time the guards were helping Anhotep to his feet, and Anhotep was protesting that what Kaffe had said was outrageous. His language was not very polite, and the guards were worried for fear Kaffe was wrong. But just in case he was right, they were keeping a tight hold on Anhotep's arms.

Then another figure staggered from the tunnel. It was Socharis. His head was bleeding and he no longer had a torch with him. He looked very grim indeed.

"Oh, Father," cried Kaffe. "You're hurt!"

But Socharis didn't seem to hear him. "Someone hit me over the head just as I stepped into the tomb chamber. He ran down the tunnel. Did you get him?" he asked the guards.

Then he saw the man they were holding between them, and when he saw who it was he sounded almost as surprised as Kaffe had been. "Anhotep!" he cried.

Anhotep did not say a word, but he began to struggle to get away, and just then Socharis swayed and crumbled up in a heap on the ground. One of the guards let go of Anhotep to help Socharis. Anhotep, seeing his chance, twisted free of the other guard and began to run toward the little sand hill where Sari had thought she saw something moving while they were waiting by the tunnel.

"Stop him! Stop him!" cried Kaffe. Sari screamed, and hearing all the noise, the guards from the litter started running toward the pyramid. The others were already chasing Anhotep, but he could run very fast, and he was frightened besides, which made him run faster. So before anyone could catch him, he had reached the sand hill and scrambled over it.

Kaffe and Sari left Anhotep to the guards. Suddenly he didn't matter, for Socharis was hurt. Kaffe was afraid his father was badly hurt, and as he knelt beside him, he forgot that he was a big boy of ten. He began to cry. Sari was crying, too. But Socharis had only fainted from the pain of the blow that Anhotep had given him, so he soon opened his eyes and tried to sit up. "What happened?" he asked.

Kaffe and Sari told him the whole story. Just as they finished, the guards came running back, but they did not bring Anhotep with them.

"He got away, Master," said one. "He had a litter waiting for him behind that sand hill over there."

"Then I did see a man's head over the top of that hill!" exclaimed Sari, and they told Socharis all about that, too.

"Which way did they go?" Socharis asked the guards.

"Out into the desert, Master," answered the guards. "We tried to catch them, but they ran like the wind."

Socharis sighed as if he was tired. "Perhaps it is just as well," he said.

"But why, Father?" asked Kaffe. "Won't he come back and rob the tomb some other time?"

Socharis shook his head. "No, Kaffe. He will not dare. We know who he is now, thanks to you and the guards, and if he ever came back to Egypt, Khufu's soldiers would surely find him."

"What would they do to him?" asked both children, their eyes round.

"What they do to all traitors," answered Socharis. "They would put him to death."

"But where will he go?" asked Sari.

"I don't know," said Socharis. "To some other country, perhaps. Anyway, we have seen the last of him. But come," he added. "We can't stay here talking all night. We must cover up that tunnel as best we can. Then we must go back to the palace and tell Khufu what has happened."

It took the guards some time to cover up the mouth of

the tunnel, but at last they brought the litter and helped Socharis in. His head had stopped bleeding and he began to feel much better. He lay back among the cushions and Kaffe and Sari crawled in beside him. Now that all the excitement was over, they felt very tired, and before they reached the edge of the valley they were sound asleep—all three of them.

9
The End of It All

When Kaffe woke up the next morning he did not know for a minute where he was. For one thing, his bed seemed to be moving, and the sun was shining in his eyes. He was just thinking of calling to Num to do something about it when he remembered where he was and what had happened. He sat up. They were already in the city, and down the street just ahead of them were the palace gates.

"Sari," cried Kaffe, "wake up! We're almost there."

Sari rubbed her eyes. For a minute she was as surprised as Kaffe had been when she saw where they were.

Socharis was still asleep, but he too awoke when the guards at the palace gate asked who they were and where they were going. He groaned a little when he sat up, but he said good morning to Kaffe and Sari very cheerfully in spite of that.

In another moment they had stepped out of the litter in front of the palace door and walked past the guards into the hall.

And there the very first person they saw was Nasha, waiting for them with Num beside her. When she saw them, Nasha cried out in dismay. Three sorrier-looking creatures than Socharis and Kaffe and Sari would have been hard to find in the whole of Egypt at that minute. Socharis' head was bound up in a strip of linen that he had torn from the edge of his kilt, and Kaffe and Sari, having slept in their clothes, looked very untidy indeed.

"What has happened to you?" asked Nasha.

"That, my dear," answered Socharis, "will take a long time to tell you. If one of the guards will let us have baths and find us some clothes and give us breakfast, I think that we can make a much better story of it than we can now."

"But you've hurt your head! Are you all right?" asked Nasha anxiously.

"Quite all right, except for a headache," answered Socharis.

Soon they were led through the palace to the room in which Kaffe and Sari were supposed to have slept, so that they might make themselves presentable before going to tell Khufu the story of their night's adventures.

"Tell me," said Socharis as they walked along behind one of Khufu's slaves, "how you happen to be here, Nasha. I sent a message to you by Num to tell you that we would not be home last night."

"That was what made me come," said Nasha. "I was sure that something was happening. I didn't know what it was, but I thought about it all night. By morning I was so curious that I sent Num for the other litter, and came to find out why you had been so mysterious. Now," she added, when the slave had left them in their room, "tell me what has happened."

So while they washed and changed their clothing and breakfasted, they told Nasha everything that had happened since they left the villa. There was so much to tell that it took a long time, and when they had finished a slave was waiting at the door to take them to Khufu.

Once more they were led out into the garden, and again they found Khufu sitting there in his carved chair, but this time he was alone. He had sent his slaves away so that he would be ready to hear their story the minute they got there.

He was very much surprised when he saw the bandage on Socharis' head. "How did this happen?" he asked. "Did you fall?" ·

Socharis smiled. "No," he answered. "I was struck."

"Struck?" asked Khufu. "Who would dare to do that?"

"The same person who dared to rob your father's tomb," replied Socharis.

Then Khufu was indeed surprised. "And have you caught the robber?" he asked.

Socharis nodded, and was just about to open his

mouth to tell Khufu who the robber was, when Kaffe interrupted. He quite forgot in his excitement that Khufu was the Pharaoh of Egypt. "Can't we start at the beginning and tell it right through to the end just as it happened?" he asked. "It makes a much better story that way."

Khufu smiled. "I think that would be a very good idea, Kaffe," he said.

"In that case," said Socharis, "Kaffe will have to begin, for I have not yet had time to find out how he and Sari happened to be under the cushions in my litter when I started from the palace."

"What? Did they go with you?" asked Khufu in amazement. "I thought they were sound asleep when you left."

"So did I," said Socharis, "but it seems that they were not. Tell us your story, Kaffe."

Kaffe was very much embarrassed, but he did as he was told. When he said that he and Sari had set off in the hope that they would meet the robbers and have a fight, he saw a twinkle in Socharis' eyes; and when he told about throwing his sandal into the courtyard to get past the guards, he saw the corners of Khufu's mouth begin to twitch; and when he reached the part about the feather's tickling his nose so that he had to sneeze, the Pharaoh and Socharis and Nasha burst out laughing.

Kaffe felt relieved. He wondered if Socharis had forgotten his promise to punish him and Sari as soon as they got back to the palace. Just in case Socharis had forgotten, Kaffe didn't think he would remind him of it.

"Now, Socharis," said Khufu when they had stopped laughing, "you go on from there." So for the second time, the story of that exciting night was told, and Khufu was a very satisfactory person to tell it to, for he exclaimed and oh-ed and ah-ed just as Nasha had when they told it to her.

"So the tomb robber was Anhotep," said Khufu thoughtfully when Socharis had finished. "It is hard for me to believe, for his father was the trusted friend of my father. Tell me," he went on, turning to Socharis, "did you suspect that it was he?"

Socharis shook his head. "No, I did not," he said, "but I should have, for everything fits together perfectly."

"What fits together?" asked Khufu.

Then Socharis had to tell the Pharaoh about their

adventures with Anhotep. He started at the very beginning and told Khufu about the day at the slave market
when Kaffe bought Sari, and how angry Anhotep was,
but how he plainly did not have enough money to pay
much for a slave girl. Then he told about the bull fight
and how surprised he had been that Anhotep was able
to buy such a fine creature as the Nubian. He told about
the night of the flood and Anhotep's rescuing the two
children and returning them to the gate of the villa in
his litter, and how Anhotep hurried off without waiting
to speak to him.

"I could not understand where he had suddenly got
so much money to spend," said Socharis. "He must have
robbed the pyramid shortly after that day at the slave
market, and sold the treasure little by little so there
would be less chance of its being noticed. I think he
looted the tomb several times. That is what he was doing last night when I found him. I saw a light in the
tomb chamber, and walked very quietly, but he must
have heard me coming. He simply stood to one side of
the door and hit me over the head as I came in. I had no
chance to see who he was, and if Kaffe hadn't tripped
him, we still wouldn't know."

"In that case," said Khufu, "I think we shall have to forgive Kaffe for going with you last night."

"Yes. As it turned out, I was very glad that he was there," agreed Socharis.

"Then you aren't going to punish us?" asked Kaffe hopefully.

"Well," said Socharis, "since you helped me so much last night, I am afraid I should seem very ungrateful if I punished you, but I shall certainly do so if you ever try anything like that again. And," he added sternly, "it will be a punishment that you will never forget."

"Yes, Father," said Kaffe. He was quite sure that Socharis meant what he said.

Then Khufu spoke. "It is I who should be ungrateful if I did not thank you for what you have done. Kaffe," he went on, "what would you like most of anything in the world if you could have it?"

Kaffe thought for a moment. Then he asked, "Do you mean something little, or something very fine?"

Khufu smiled. "Oh, something very fine, of course," he said.

It did not take Kaffe long to make up his mind. "I'd like a dagger," he said. "A real dagger that I can use when I grow up. That's what I meant to get with my fourteen copper rings the day I bought Sari instead," he explained.

"A dagger?" asked Khufu. "Well, that at least is something that will be useful for a long time to come." He clapped his hands, and when a slave appeared, he whispered something to him. When the man had run off, he turned to Socharis.

"I have a plan in my head for Kaffe," he said. "It seems to me that it is time he came to the palace to have his lessons with my children as you did with my brothers and me in my father's time."

Socharis and Nasha were very much pleased. It was an honor to be asked to go to school at the palace. Before this, Kaffe had had his lessons at home.

As for Kaffe, he didn't know for a few minutes whether he liked the idea or not. "Would I have to live here at the palace all the time?" he asked, trying not to think as he said it how much he would miss the villa and his father and mother and Sari.

"No," answered Khufu gently. "Not all the time. You would spend all the holidays at home, and you could go home any other time you cared to besides. We don't want to take you away from your family, but we do want you to come to like us here at the palace."

"Then I should like to come," said Kaffe. "I suppose that Sari will have to stay at home," he added.

"I'll tell you what I shall do," said Nasha. "While you are here at the palace, I shall teach Sari all the things that girls need to know how to do. She will be going to school just as you are, and whenever you come home, she will be there to play with you just as she is now."

Sari bowed her head. "Oh, thank you, Mistress," she said. She thought she was very lucky, for it was not often that a slave was taken into the house and taught by a great lady like Nasha.

After that, it seemed to Kaffe and Sari that nothing more wonderful could happen, but they soon found out that it could. A little procession of slaves marched into the garden. There were four of them, and when Kaffe and Sari saw what they were carrying, their eyes grew as big as saucers.

First of all came a slave bearing a tall golden vase set with lapis lazuli. It flashed and glittered so in the sunlight that it made the children blink to look at it. Khufu took the lovely thing in his hands and said to Socharis, "Because you have been a faithful friend, I want to give you this vase for your tomb. Your loyalty is worth a hundred such vases, but I have only this one to give you. Please accept it with my gratitude."

When Socharis had thanked him, Khufu took a length of fine white linen from the second slave. This he gave to Nasha. Then he came to the third slave, and took from him something flat and shiny that he held out on the palms of both hands. When Kaffe saw what it was, he gasped, for it was the most beautiful dagger he had ever seen. It had a bright gold hilt decorated with blue, red and green enamel, and a sharp copper blade that flashed in the sun as Khufu held it up.

"This is for you, Kaffe," said Khufu. "I had it made as a present for my eldest son, but I can have another made for him. I want you to have this, for you too have helped me, and I think I can trust you always to use it wisely."

Kaffe was so overcome that he could only stammer, "Oh, thank you, sir," but Khufu knew how he felt, and he smiled.

Last of all, he took from the fourth slave a little string of turquoise beads and held them out to Sari. "These are for you, little Sari," he said. "You have been a faithful slave, and such loyalty is something we cannot do without."

After they had said good-bye to Khufu, and had thanked him again, Socharis, Nasha, Kaffe and Sari started off in their litters toward their own villa.

When they were home once more, sitting in their own garden, Socharis said, "Now I know what I am going to have painted on the other wall of my mastaba."

"What is that?" asked Nasha.

"Why," said Socharis, "the story of what has happened ever since that day we went to the slave market in Memphis."

"Oh, Father," cried Kaffe, "will I be there, and Sari and Red Boy and Anhotep and everything?"

Sari clapped her hands.

"Yes, indeed," said Socharis. "Every bit of the story, even to Red Boy's chasing you two up the fig tree."

And that is just what he did, so perhaps if you should go to Gizeh today, and could find the mastaba that Socharis built, you might see there, painted on the wall, the very pictures that tell this story.

CPSIA information can be obtained at www.ICGtesting.com
Printed in the USA
BVOW030954220513

321361BV00010B/435/P